Understanding
Today's
Theatre

Understanding Today's Theatre

Cinema · Stage · Television

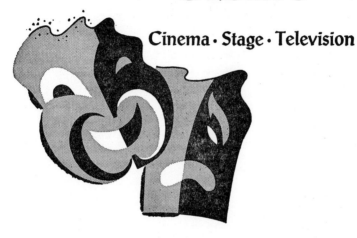

Edward A. Wright
DENISON UNIVERSITY

A SPECTRUM  BOOK

PRENTICE-HALL, INC.

LIBRARY OF CONGRESS
CATALOG CARD NO.: 59–15642

First printing ...... November, 1959
Second printing ... September, 1960
Third printing .... December, 1961
Fourth printing .... July, 1962

PRINTED IN THE UNITED STATES OF AMERICA

93622-C

Preface

Understanding Today's Theatre is directed to the audience—that wonderful, unpredictable, and indispensable participant in any dramatic production on stage or screen.

For those in the audience who have little or no dramatic background, these pages explain some basic principles that have proved themselves over the centuries and some facts and opinions on the theatre as a synthesis of the arts. A special effort has been made to help the audience distinguish the substance, form, and technique of the various artists involved in any dramatic production.

Thirty-seven years of active participation on both sides of the footlights, with the commercial and noncommercial theatre, have given birth to many convictions, two of which are that audience attitudes can be altered—most theatregoers are anxious and willing to learn more about why they did or did not enjoy a specific experience—and that the ideal playgoer is a happy combination of intelligence and innocence. He knows and appreciates both theatre and literary values; he respects—even reveres—the theatre and what it can be.

References to specific plays or personal experiences have been kept to a minimum in the hope that the reader will apply the material to the TV, motion picture, or stage production he saw last night, or last week, and arrive at his own estimate of its values, artistic or otherwise.

Remember, however, that in the theatre, as in life, education consists of learning the rules; experience teaches the exceptions.

EDWARD A. WRIGHT

Granville, Ohio

Contents

Understanding Today's Theatre

O N E

A theatrical approach

Do you, in your theatre-going, ask for escape, stimulation, excitement, entertainment, or enjoyment? Have you ever wondered why you were or were not affected by a television, movie, or stage program—or why your friends had a completely different reaction? Can you distinguish between the work of the actor and the director? Did you ever stop to ask yourself what the author or costumer, cameraman, scene-designer—even the audience itself—had contributed to the total effect of a dramatic production? Is last night's or last week's—or last year's—show on television, movie screen, or stage still alive in your memory? Would you make an effort to see it again, or advise someone else to do so? Why?

This book will try to help you answer just such questions, for it is directed to you as one of the 110,000,000 to 120,000,000 Americans who made up last night's theatre audience in the homes and theatres across the country. Whether it was on a television or motion picture screen, an educational, community, or professional stage, you were part of that theatre production—in many respects the most vital part. You were an active participant in one of the oldest institutions of mankind—the theatre—which is today playing a greater part in our daily lives than at any previous time in all history. You were consciously or unconsciously evaluating the work and the art of all those men and women who had given their best to that performance, who were working for your entertainment, escape, enjoyment, or whatever else you might demand of a theatre performance.

Are you qualified to give an honest or an intelligent judgment of their work? It is the purpose of these pages to help you do just that; to assist you in formulating some honest standard of dramatic criticism; to set forth some basic principles that will bring about a fairer evaluation of the work of all the artists involved, and ultimately to make you a better theatregoer who will demand a finer dramatic fare—and this will in turn create a more intelligent theatre audience.

The theatre is a *popular* (in all its etymological implications) art, and most theatre workers would consider you, the audience, as both their master and their teacher, if not the very reason for the theatre's existence. You are that giant who stands at the box office or stays away; who turns on or turns off the TV switch and who—alone—determines whether or not a dramatic production will continue, or whether a given program stays on the air. It is you who builds the performer's reputation and establishes the popularity of the theatre personality. The great stars of our theatre world stand in more awe of you, the audience, than do you of their prominence, for you are the one who makes that prominence. You will decide when he or she has become a "has been" as well as when he or she rises to stardom. Without your approval a theatre closes, millions of dollars are lost, artists are discarded.

What have you done, or what can you do to merit such power and authority? Many will shrug off such a question with the familiar, "I know what I like," or "All I want is my money's worth." Greater truth lies in a slight alteration of these phrases so that they become, "I like what I know," and "I get more for my money when I know *why* I have (or have not) got my money's worth." In other words, it may not be nearly as important for you, as an individual, to have liked or disliked a work of art as it is for you, a person of intelligence, to know why you did or did not approve, and also to understand why others have or have not done so.

At any rate, it is our purpose in *Understanding Today's Theatre* figuratively to go backstage and see something of the art and work that goes into the writing of the story, the acting of the roles, the contributions of the various technicians, and director.

SOME BASIC ASSUMPTIONS

Before beginning that backstage journey there are some basic assumptions that we must establish as a background or foundation for our discussion.

We shall assume that the word *theatre* today includes television, motion pictures, and stage. Even though the stage is attended by far fewer theatregoers than either of the other two mediums, it is the parent of them both. In its long history the stage has established many principles and traditions to which the two younger children must adhere. The camera is by far the greatest single difference between the parent and her offspring. Not only has it made these two mediums the theatre of the masses, but with it has come many new techniques. In the appropriate chapters these differences will be pointed out and discussed.

We would emphasize that a complete mastery of the following pages will not guarantee dramatic appreciation, for appreciation in itself cannot be taught. It is only a by-product that comes with knowledge and experience. It is our belief, however, that *taste* can be improved, and improving one's taste is a long step toward appreciation. We would define taste as a mental perception of quality, a perception embodying *judgment,* a discriminative faculty—the act of liking or preferring something—and the *sense of what is appropriate, harmonious, or beautiful* in nature or art. Both taste and judgment will always be relative and our goal is not to dictate a number of artistic *fiats,* but, rather, to improve, in some way, the general taste of the reader so far as his dramatic fare is concerned. While we are convinced that public feelings are rarely reversed, we do feel that there is within any entertainment medium the power to extend or retard the desires or demands of its audience.

A third basic assumption and cornerstone of our approach to the whole area of theatre is that the word *theatricalism* is part of any theatrical experience.

The meaning of this term is at once obvious. It implies exaggeration, something overdone, life or nature *theatricalized* and as such it usually carries a negative connotation. Some writers choose to use the word *magnification* and thus partially avoid such a reaction.

We would prefer to consider this very essential factor in all theatre production in a thoroughly positive sense and define theatricalism as *exaggeration under control*. When used with taste and discrimination, it supplies a spirit or quality that enhances every phase of the production. When misused or uncontrolled it is not only a distraction, but can destroy any admirable ideas, emotions or qualities the production may wish to emphasize.

All theatre is exaggeration, for it must emphasize and project what it is trying to say. Theatre must be bigger than life if it is to reach an audience. Merely finding the truth is not enough. Reality must be interpreted and expressed in a distinctive way.

Many of us today feel that our modern theatre, with its great emphasis on realism, has lost much of its power because too many of its workers and some of its audiences hold too great a fear of the theatrical and look upon it as a plague rather than the very soul of the theatre which it can and should be.

Walter Kerr, New York critic, has very aptly expressed this theme:

"Theatrical" has, in this day and age, very nearly become a dirty word. We have been obsessed with naturalistic stage deportment for so long that we have got ourselves into the paradoxical position of insisting that the theatre be as untheatrical as possible. We have become suspicious of any voice raised above a whisper, or any gesture more emphatic than that required to light a cigarette, of any facial display beyond the casually raised eyebrow. An overt performance seems to be a dishonest one, a mere ragbag of tricks employed by a calculating actor to conceal his interior poverty. In our enthusiasm for the "realistic" method, we have come to equate sincerity with low gear.*

* Walter Kerr, "Don Juan in Hell," *New York Herald Tribune*, November 4, 1951.

4

The goal of all theatre has been to give what Aristotle called an imitation of an action. That very word "imitation" means that what the audience sees can never be literally the real thing; something must have been altered. That something is the artist's personality, imagination and creativeness. It is this addition that distinguishes theatre from life.

Even in our most modern and realistic theatre the language used by the playwright, the settings that would attempt to portray locale, the lighting that strives for realism and the acting that would portray all emotions and movements in the most literal and life-like manner must use artifice or techniques that can only give an illusion of life rather than life itself. The audience is always conscious of being in a theatre or at least viewing an imagined situation rather than a real one. Both artist and audience are well aware that this theatre-audience-artist combination creates a relationship very different from the circumstances that would exist in real life. The result is an imitation of life and involves theatricalism, or exaggeration under control.

The emotions experienced in life and those experienced in the theatre are essentially the same. The methods of obtaining and expressing those emotions and the effects they have on both artist and audience are vastly different. Mr. Gassner has defined these two elements as life's reality and theatrical reality. He defines the latter as making the most of all the theatre's elements rather than trying to hide or deny them.

Vaudeville, musical comedy, the circus, the opera, and the works of Shakespeare, Molière, and the Greeks never abandoned their theatricality. The clown, Pierrot, Pierrette, Charles Chaplin's creations, Hamlet, Oedipus, and Tartuffe are supreme examples of theatricalism. Their emotions are just as real as are the emotions of Willy Loman or the protagonist in a motion picture or television melodrama. Each is theatrical in its own way and in harmony with the dramatic event of which it is a part.

One can say things in a play he could not say in any other way—because we know it is "make-believe." Through the arts we can

permeate all iron curtains whether set up by politicians, by igno-
rance, or by provincialism. It is the very theatricality of the theatre
that makes it so real. The actor can get away with the truth because
he does not mean it. Our guard is down.

It is this essential theatricality that has made Charles Chaplin,
Danny Kaye, and Bob Hope the most influential ambassadors this
country has ever had.

In each of our theatre mediums today there are many artists—
playwrights, actors, designers, and directors—who have each in
their own way used theatricalism advantageously. Occasionally the
motion pictures and television screens have given us productions
which have been like a breath of fresh air to those of us almost
suffocated by the surface realism that would seem to deny the
theatre's theatricality. To recognize and appreciate the artistry of
those who have successfully given us emotional truth through
theatrical reality is no small part of the drama critic's responsibility.

SOURCES OF INFORMATION

The requisites of any good dramatic critic must include some
knowledge of the theatre and dramatic history, a sense of theatre
and an appreciation of its possibilities, some honest standard of
theatre evaluation that includes both taste and discrimination, and
an understanding of the form and techniques involved in the work
of each theatre artist.

Our search for theatre knowledge, understanding, and background is dependent upon three sources of information—facts,
principles, and opinions.

Facts

Facts are quite easily recognized. They may consist of historical
data, the names and contributions of playwrights, dramas, actors,
technicians, the stories of plays, definitions of terms, and so on, and
on. Many would consider this historical background essential to any

effective or honest dramatic criticism. For example, the following five statements are facts:

1. The motion pictures are less than seventy-five years of age, and television less than twenty-five, but the stage has been an important part of and influence on our western civilization for more than three thousand years.

2. Our theatre in England and America has its origin in the life of the Greeks where it was part of their religious service some five hundred years before Christ; and Sophocles, Aeschylus, Euripides, and Aristophanes were four of the greatest Greek playwrights.

3. The Elizabethan Age in England, during the latter part of the sixteenth century and very early part of the seventeenth, was one of the greatest literary eras of the English speaking peoples, and William Shakespeare was its leader; *Hamlet* is considered by many to be the greatest play ever written in English and it tells the story of a young man who discovers that his father has been murdered by his uncle and that his mother is now married to the murderer.

4. Henrik Ibsen, a Norwegian, is considered to be the father of the modern drama; he wrote his greatest plays between 1860 and 1905, and he was the author of such social plays as *The Doll's House, Ghosts,* and *Hedda Gabler* which were most effective in bringing about a change in both our attitude toward life and the very laws of our land.

5. More people in this country can say on any given morning, "I saw a play last night" than at any time in history, for 84 per cent of our American homes have television sets, and between 40,000,000 and 80,000,000 persons attend the motion pictures every week—in addition to thousands of stage productions by school, community, and professional groups across the country.

Principles

Our second source of information is more difficult, for principles are often variable and frequently open to question, debate, or change. The individual may accept a principle now and, later, discard it altogether. A principle is a specific point of view or conviction from which we make our start in analyzing a given piece of work, a sort of springboard in our thinking, or the soil out of which grows our ultimate opinion. Eventually these beliefs become a part of us and are the sub-strata which determines our taste and finally our appreciation. The fact that certain principles are found in these pages does not imply that they are the final answer, nor that the reader must accept them. It does mean that they are precepts upon which the author has arrived at his own opinions or conclusions in dramatic criticism. They can be helpful to the reader as the first step in building his own standard of evaluation, especially if he chooses to accept them until he has discovered some that he likes better. They can for the present become the anchors that any beginner so often needs. It is important to remember, however, that no principle is of more value than the integrity of the individual who applies it.

We now present six basic principles or beliefs that have become fundamental in our particular approach to theatre understanding and dramatic criticism. These precepts are quite generally accepted in the field of dramatic criticism and have become established over many years. Each principle should be kept in mind as the following pages are read, for they are the bedrock upon which any of our opinions are founded.

Principle Number 1: That Goethe's three questions—"What is the artist trying to do?" "How well has he done it?" and "Is it worth the doing?"—furnish a valid premise to any artistic evaluation.

As the very corner-stone of our whole approach to art appreciation, as the premise to every decision we shall make regarding the work of any artist in or out of the theatre, we cannot emphasize too strongly the validity and the importance of this first principle which we have borrowed from the works of the great German playwright, philosopher and critic, Johann Wolfgang von Goethe (1739-1832). Whether we are evaluating the work of playwright, actor, scene-designer, electrician, costumer, cameraman, or director, every artist has the inalienable right to express himself as he may desire. We may not agree that it is best; we may not like what he says, his point of view, his form of expression, or his style, but it is his right to work as he chooses, and we should as observers ask ourselves the three questions:

What is the artist trying to do? Is he writing a farce, a melodrama, a tragedy or a comedy? Is his goal sheer escape or would he teach us some great lesson? Is this purely a commercial venture or an effort at an artistic production? Are the actors attempting to create characters or to be themselves and merely comment on the role? What is the over-all purpose of the production?

How well has he done it? This is the critic's opportunity to place his judgment on the degree of success the artist has attained in his efforts. Here we evaluate his technique, his methods, his success in attaining the goals he has set up for himself. We are now concerned with the over-all effectiveness of the work of each artist and of the whole production, and that effectiveness is measured by the *principles* that we or others have chosen to be the yardsticks of our dramatic knowledge. In a given area these principles may become a part of the artist's form (see *Principle 3*).

Is it worth the doing? Once again the goal of the artist is brought into focus, but now we raise the question of value in time and effort on the part of both artist and viewer. A completely new approach or end may have been presented. The artist may or may not have succeeded in arriving at his goal. We, as the audience, must now say whether or not we feel the end or the means to that end were worth while, and our conclusions may be called *opinions.*

Due recognition of these three questions will help us to avoid the pitfall of most amateur critics. Too often the novice condemns a motion picture in his effort to compare it with a stage production, or vice versa. He deplores the dramatic program on television without asking why. He bemoans the frothiness of an inconsequential farce because it does not have the stature of a more serious play. He sometimes stands in awe of a dramatic piece built on a most ambitious scale, though it has not been adequately executed by the artist. Again, he frowns upon the very thought of melodrama or farce instead of weighing each in the light of certain accepted principles laid down for farce or for melodrama. By answering Goethe's questions, we can escape the common error of condemning or praising without an evaluation of the artist's conception, the medium, the technique, and the values involved.

Principle Number 2: That art may be defined as life reflected by or interpreted through a personality.

Man is not limited to the things he can see, hear, or touch. Unlike other animals he has the power of picturing in his mind what is not, but what might be. He is able not only to accumulate, record and profit by the experiences of the past, but with his imagination to devise new ways of doing things—in short, to have new ideas.

Francis Bacon once said: "Art is man added to nature," and the moment that man enters the situation we have the element of selection and emphasis rather than sheer representation, for man interprets, and no two persons see exactly the same picture.

A common practice is to confuse the two words *reality* and *realism*. Reality is life "for real." Realism is an illusion of life as portrayed by the artist—life as "make-believe." No artist is ever wholly natural—he only *seems* natural. The most interesting conversation in life would be unreal or unsatisfactory in the theatre, lacking emphasis, coherence, unity, climax, or continuity. The very characters we might shun in life are frequently found to be most delightful or entertaining on the stage. All art implies selection on the part of the artist. A photograph is artistic only when the element of choice is evident through the subject chosen, through its arrangement, the lighting, the emphasis, and even through the delicate touches obtained in the development and re-touching of the negative.

Let us imagine, for a moment, that an individual has had an experience in life which has given him great personal pleasure by affecting him either emotionally or intellectually. It may have been the discovery of a great truth, the realization of a philosophy, the beauty of a sunset, the song of a bird, or some humorous or serious aspect of daily life. In any event, the participant has an all-consuming desire to reproduce that experience so that it can be shared with others. He must first choose the art through which he will speak. What he wants to share may be most easily expressed by the dance, by a musical composition, a poem, the painting of a picture, the drawing of a cartoon. He could choose the short story, the novel, or the drama. Let us further imagine that he has chosen the drama. Readers of this drama may find in it what the playwright has meant to say or they may even discover some further experience of their own which they, too, wish to share. They produce the drama which then becomes a play, and they, in turn, become the actors who interpret the characters, the technicians who create the scenery, costumes, lighting, and other theatrical effects, and the director, the leader who envisions and supervises the whole production. In the work of each artist will appear some facet of his own thinking, feeling, and background, for the tree an artist paints is not nature's tree —it is his. The characters a playwright creates are not life's characters—they are his. St. Joan, Queen Elizabeth, Abraham Lincoln, Mary of Scotland have appeared countless times in literature. Each creation is different, though patterned after the same model, for each is the sum total of the author's impression, technique, and imagination. In the art of acting, twenty Hamlets will be twenty different people, though they speak the same lines, for each actor must create the character through his own experiences and personality. Every artist selects and emphasizes just what he desires us, his audience, to see, for we see life through his eyes. The playwright tells his story within his own chosen framework with characters, dialogue, and theme all slanted to portray life as he sees it. The actor creates the role in terms of his own physical, emotional, vocal, and intellectual qualifications. The various technicians do that which must be done to sustain the mood, project the story, and enhance the production, while the director as a creator, interpreter, and coordinator, translates all these elements into a single and harmonious whole. All work with a single goal—to share an emotional experience by portraying a reflection of life through their own personality and in the hope of bringing to the audience a memorable experience.

In art, we who make up the audience are given the opportunity of new and varied experiences, of momentarily stepping out of our own little world of reality and knowing the worlds that are inhabited by the great artists of the world, past and present. We look, for the moment, at life through their eyes and their personalities.

Through art we may become acquainted with a whole new world from the one we know. Brooks Atkinson has said this most effectively in the following quotation:

Out of his imagination, exultancy, despair, revolt or passion the artist creates a world that has his own coherence and submits it as the truth. For the worlds of art are bewilderingly unalike. The tragic world of Sophocles, the tender, reverent world of Michelangelo, the gamy world of Chaucer, Shakespeare's vast world of intelligence and sensibility, the satirical world of Molière, the human world of Dickens, the mad world of Van Gogh, and the luminous world of Manet, the noble world of Beethoven, and the nervous world of Stravinsky, the electric world of Shaw, the dark world of O'Neill, the gusty world of O'Casey—these are some of the worlds available.*

Principle Number 3. That art consists of three specific elements—substance, form, and technique—and that an understanding of each element is necessary for honest criticism.

Substance is essentially what the artist is trying to say—his subject, the material of his creation, the aspect of life which he wishes to communicate or share with his audience.

Form is the particular art in which he has chosen to speak, the shape or structure within which he will create. It involves the accepted principles in that medium, for, while rules must never confine art, art does consistently produce rules. Almost one hundred years after the great playwrights of Greece had written their masterpieces, Aristotle studied them and then wrote his *Poetics* in which he presented the basic principles of playwriting. For centuries these principles were the guides for playwrights.

It was not until Shakespeare, and later Ibsen, broke this classic

* Brooks Atkinson, "Note On Art," *The New York Times*, Sept. 8, 1957.

form that new boundaries or dramatic principles came into existence. It must constantly be emphasized that each artist always has the right of casting aside the accepted forms and creating a new one of his own. The only requirement is that the results must be equally as—or more—effective than they would have been with the generally accepted form which he has forsaken.

Technique is the method of fitting or blending the substance into the form. It is the artist's personal means of accomplishing his end and involves the selection and arrangement of his materials for a particular effect. Form and technique are the elements that differentiate art from life, and technique, in addition, is the element which distinguishes one artist's work from that of another. It is sometimes called his personal style or quality, for it is essentially the artist's projection of himself. The three mediums—stage, motion picture, and television—are very much alike so far as substance and form are concerned, but they vary greatly in their techniques.

A popular melody may be played in twenty different ways by as many orchestras. The same view never looks exactly the same when painted or drawn by several artists. Two actors could not possibly play a role the same, nor could two playwrights write the same story in the same way, though both of them may be dealing with the same subject and following the same principles—principles dictated by the form in which that subject has been interpreted.

Alexandre Dumas, *fils*, the French playwright, once said: "Technique is so important that it sometimes happens that technique is mistaken for art." We are all familiar with those personalities on the stage or in motion pictures or television who depend too much on their technique or showmanship for success. Such artists usually have a very short professional life, for substance and form are in the final analysis more important. Technique without something to say is not enough. In the chapters dealing with the playwright, the actors, the technicians, and the director, we shall further distinguish between these three components of an art, for it is fundamental to our premise that the dramatic critic must have some knowledge of the various forms and techniques common to drama and theatre production, both past and present. Then, and only then, can he competently and fairly answer the three questions of Goethe.

Principle Number 4: That the purpose of art is to give aesthetic pleasure and to clarify life through the communication of the artist's thoughts, ideas, or emotions to his audience.

It is the primary function of any work of art to stimulate the imagination through the senses. The physical experience of beauty lifts us out of ourselves and enables us to see more deeply into the great realities. This has been called aesthetic pleasure and is defined as an appreciation of the beautiful. Just what beauty is has never been absolutely defined. It may be different things to different people. There are those who feel that beauty is inherent in the subject matter itself and that the artist merely records that beauty. There are others who believe that beauty lies in the artist's skill, style, or technique in duplicating nature. Some would call it a "unity in variety" or the complete harmony of all the elements that the artist has used to express a central idea or theme.

Many moderns contend that beauty exists in the mind of the viewer or hearer, that the artist strikes some note which brings to the observer's mind a pleasurable experience or emotion that gives the aesthetic pleasure through recognition of a past experience. Still another theory would place the sense of beauty in the artist's personal interpretation of what he sees. This has given us both the *impressionist* and the *expressionist* as well as the many "isms" of modern art.

There are also some who would unite their ethical or religious thinking with their aesthetic sense. They are the followers of John Keats and his belief that "Beauty is truth, truth beauty." Closely allied, but standing by themselves, are those who insist that only the presence of God or an emphasis on their own moral code combined with their art can give them aesthetic pleasure. In the theatre these individuals are often called the moralists, for they insist upon the presence of a great moral theme or lesson.

Then there are the intellectuals who insist that, before any art

14

object can give them aesthetic pleasure, it must challenge them to think, or give them a greater understanding of the world's problems. It is the contention of this book that there is just as much beauty in our theatre today as at any time in all history. We would not for a moment be classed with those pessimists who feel that the theatre is dying or those who constantly cry for the "good old days" and protest that "the theatre is not what it used to be." We agree with the man who said that poetry is present at that moment when one becomes conscious of the presence of the beautiful. By such a definition poetry certainly did not go out of the theatre with the death of Shakespeare or Jonson. It has only changed its emphasis. In many respects there is more poetry in our modern theatre than was present in Shakespeare's day. His poetry lay in the written text of the play; ours lies in the complete harmony of all the arts that are found in a dramatic production.

Historically the Greeks sought their poetry in the dialogue. For the Mediaevalists it was found in the theme of the liturgical play, expressing to the masses in understandable language the Biblical stories the priests could not give them in Latin. The Renaissance in Italy found it in the scenic, dramatic backgrounds of Leonardo da Vinci and other contemporary artists; the English, in the incomparable language of Shakespeare; the French, in the superb pantomime of the *commedia dell' arte* which finally emerged in Molière's comedy of manners. The realists have found it in the completeness of their artistic representation of life on the stage. The expressionist finds it in the imaginativeness of his conception. Thus all have found beauty in the theatre, whether it be in the acting, the direction, the setting, the story itself, the work of the technicians, or as it is today, the theatre offers beauty in the harmonious coordination of all these contributing artists.

Closely allied to the importance of aesthetic pleasure is the second phase of this fourth principle: the clarity of the artist's communication. On this subject we are in complete agreement with the following two quotations. The first is from Count Leo Tolstoy who has said:

Art is a human activity which is passed on to others, causing them to feel and experience what the artist has felt and experienced . . . It is a means of communication between people, uniting them in the same feelings . . . As soon as the spectators and the hearers are affected by the same feelings which the artist felt—that is art.

The second is from Aristotle who wrote: "The aim of art is to represent not the outward appearance of things, but their inward significance; for this, and not the external mannerism and detail, is true reality."

Art, then, should clarify and not further complicate life. It is wholly possible that we may differ with the artist's opinion, his interpretation of life or his conclusions. We may not like the way in which he has portrayed his feelings or thoughts; we may question the values involved or whether or not they should have been expressed, but we should be clear as to the artist's purpose, his feelings and his thoughts. We should know, personally, what he has been trying to say. This does not mean that someone else may not get from the work another idea or a different emotional response. Our backgrounds, our point of view, our mental processes are so different that we may frequently interpret the same art work differently from others.

This clarity of communication is even more important in the theatre, for there the actors and director must have corrected any doubt that may have been left by the playwright. A play should be a movement toward something. For an audience to leave the theatre without a clear idea of what that something is or not to know what the play is about is indefensible. The duty of art is to clarify life—not further to confuse or complicate it.

Clayton Hamilton has further emphasized this principle in the following quotation:

Art and Nature compete eternally with each other in the great task of making humanity aware of what is true and beautiful and good. They are the two teachers in our schoolroom of a world . . . It would be difficult to judge decisively whether Art or Nature is the greater teacher. Nature has more to tell us, but Art is better skilled for utterance. Nature has so much to say that she has no patience for articulation. She thrills us with a vague awareness of multitudinous indecipherable messages; but she speaks to us in whispers and in thunders—elusive, indeterminate, discomforting. Art, with less to say, has more patience for the formulation of her messages; she speaks to us in a voice that has been deliberately trained, and her utterance is lucid and precise. She does not try, like Nature, to tell us everything at once. She selects, instead, some single definite and little truth to tell us at a time, and exerts herself to speak it clearly. We can never estimate precisely what it is that we have learned from Naure; but whatever Art has spoken to us, we know exactly what we have been told.*

Principle Number 5: That the theatre is a meeting ground or synthesis of all the arts and as such consists of five areas—play, actors, technicians, director, and audience, each of which must be properly evaluated before the whole production has been seen.

For many years the fine arts were considered to include the dance, music, poetry or literature, sculpture, painting, drawing, and architecture. Some of the more recent publications of standard dictionaries have listed an eighth—dramatic art. Whether or not this becomes common practice is unimportant, for even a casual analysis of the elements that compose the seven fine arts will point up the fundamental truth that the theatre is perhaps the one place where all the elements of all the arts meet on common ground— the *bodily movement* and *gesture* of the dance, the *rhythm, melody,* and *harmony* of music, the *meter* and *words* of literature, and the *line, mass,* and *color* of the space arts—sculpture, painting, drawing and architecture. Surely, then, the theatre is a synthesis of the arts, if not an art in itself. With today's emphasis on the total dramatic production and the unification of all its elements, the theatre, whether an art or as a synthesis of the arts, is subject to the tests of unity, emphasis, rhythm, balance, proportion, harmony and grace which will be further discussed in Chapter Five.

This is a book on *theatre* rather than *drama* understanding. The drama, or written script, is only one part of a theatre production. There are many non-literary elements involved in the play. The

* Clayton Hamilton, *Theory of the Theatre* (New York: Henry Holt & Co., 1939).

crafts, as well as the arts, become important ingredients as the actors, technicians, director, and audience are brought into the total picture. It takes many elements to make a play, and it is made for many people. The written script is only a drama and does not become a play until it is performed on a stage, by actors and before an audience. The theatre is a genuinely cooperative art.

The theatre today—if not from its very beginning—is in effect a five-ring circus. Until all five rings have been seen and evaluated, we have not really seen the production. These five areas include the playwright, the actors, the technicians, the director, and the audience. In many respects you, the audience, are the most important of all the contributors, for the others—author, actors, technicians, and director—have from the beginning been working for your satisfaction, your approval, your enjoyment or entertainment.

These areas, and all they imply, are the elements of the theatre. Until the theatregoer has recognized and honestly judged the contributions of every artist involved, he has not really seen the play.

Principle Number 6: That the theatre—as an art—has specific obligations to its audience, and the audience—as part of the total dramatic production—has specific obligations to the theatre.

The theatre must always make its appeal to the *audience* rather than to the individual. This very fact broadens the meaning of beauty and emphasizes our conviction that art, and certainly the theatre, must never resort to the oft-quoted phrase, "art for art's sake." It is a maxim of this book that such a statement is utterly without validity. The theatre is the possession of all the people and should exist for and speak to them.

Those artists of the theatre who would write or produce for themselves or their own little group and who look down upon the "common people" are but drawing the cloak of oblivion over the art they profess to love. This responsibility need never discourage experimentation, growth, and change. On the contrary, it may give them birth, for audiences are willing to learn and are ever seeking something new. History has shown them to be both receptive and easily adapted to change, but the theatre artist, more than any other, may be compelled to move more slowly. At least, he must never forget that he is the servant of the crowd.

The true lover of the theatre considers it a democratic institution that belongs fundamentally to the people. He would criticize just as severely the producers or directors who cater to the lower dramatic taste and conceive the theatre to exist only as escape as he would those who would sacrifice entertainment and cry out for only intellectual drama or theatre with a message. One is as much in error as the other. The first may talk of "giving them what they want" and "show business," while the other cries out for "art theatre" or "social significance." The former demands nothing of his audience, and the latter asks too much. Eventually both are doomed to failure, for each is soon faced by a disappointed and steadily diminishing audience.

Someone has divided the theatre audience into three extremes—the escapists, the moralists, and the artsakists. First, there are the escapists who want only to forget the responsibilities and problems of their everyday life. They ask only to be amused and clamor only for the lighter plays or musicals. They are referred to as the "tired business men," although they are found in all professions and sometimes, surprisingly enough, among our most brilliant minds.

Not long after *Death of a Salesman* had completed its road tour, a professor from a large university was heard to condemn that play because it had haunted him for days, and he seemed not to be able to put it out of his mind. When asked why he had not liked the play, his answer was: "It had nothing to say." Those within hearing were quick to point out that it said a great deal with its theme showing that a man who builds his life and that of his family on a foundation that is both shallow and ethically unsound will be doomed to failure. The professor readily agreed that he had found all that in the play but that what troubled him was that there were too many people exactly like that in America. This was an even more astonishing revelation, for it meant that he had completely shut his eyes and mind to the fact that people might sense the theme and realize their own errors, at least the younger generation, before it was too late. Then came the answer that should have been foreseen had it not come from so distinguished an educator: "To tell you the truth, when I go to the theatre, I want something light and entertaining."

What even this professor did not realize was that "entertain" need not only mean amuse, for it is derived from the Latin word, *tenere* which means "to hold." Consequently, tragedy may be equally as entertaining as farce. What he meant was that his only demand so far as the theatre was concerned was "escape." This first group—unfortunately a very large one—may be called the *escapists*.

The second group includes those who demand that the theatre must always uplift, teach a lesson, preach a sermon, picture some part of life of which they personally approve. They would close their eyes to anything with which they do not agree, and insist that only "beautiful and nice clean plays be presented." We find these persons in every community, and they are one of the greatest problems which the director in the non-commercial theatre must face. Either they blind themselves to the fact that evil does exist in the world, or they refuse to accept the theatre as a reflection of life. In either instance, they are being honest neither with themselves nor with the artists whom they would criticize. This group we may call the *moralists*.

The third extreme is made up of those theatregoers who insist on "art for art's sake." They shudder at box-office success, and disdainfully refer to all popular theatre as "show business." They deny that the theatre belongs to the people and would claim it for their own little esoteric group. They smugly infer that popularity with an audience is only an ingredient of mediocrity and far beneath the true artist. These individuals, whom we call the *artsakists*, like to think of themselves as intellectuals.

To please these three extremes and the millions who lie between is not an easy task, but they all make up that audience out front for whom every theatre artist is working. In *The Art of Playgoing* John Mason Brown says:

Stand at the entrance to any theatre when the audience is assembling; look into its multitudinous face; study its varying expressions; attempt to gauge the separate minds which are mere cells in its composite brain; think of the conflicting interests, perceptions, backgrounds, vocabularies, sympathies, standards, convictions, consciences, and levels of sophistication from which his giant body is sprung, and the challenges and difficulties faced by dramatists in presenting such situations, ideas, and characters as will be comprehensible and acceptable to the crowd even when they are satisfactorily meeting our own quite different individual demands will be made clearer for us than any textbook or dramatic technique has ever been able to make them.*

The variety of what this audience may most appreciate is unlimited. Some may desire the lines of Sophocles or Shakespeare, and others, the lines of today's most popular motion picture actress. One may choose a play that propagandizes some religious or social theme, and another an historical romance or biography. To some a line of pretty chorus girls backed by spectacular scenery and accompanied by lively music may have a far greater appeal than the latest tragedy by Miller or poetic drama by T. S. Eliot. One may clamor for revivals of the classics or a dramatization of a famous novel, while his neighbor would prefer the naturalness of Chekhov or the repartee of Noel Coward. There are always those in attendance who would find their greatest pleasure in the preachments of Shaw, the epic theatre of Brecht, the searchings of Pirandello, the time relativity or fourth dimensional philosophy of J. B. Priestley, or the intellectual challenge demanded of the theatre by Eric Bentley. Practically every theatre audience will include some shading of all these individuals.

Secondly, it is our contention that the audience goes to the theatre to be moved emotionally and that the theatre is first a chapel of emotion; the audience may be surprised, stirred, excited, amused, frightened, saddened or thrilled—the emotional content is more important, fundamentally, than the intellectual. If the ex-

* John Mason Brown, *The Art of Playgoing* (New York: W. W. Norton & Company, Inc., 1936).

perience can teach a truth of life, inspire the audience to do finer things, thrill them with its poetry or literary quality, send them out better equipped to face life, or challenge them intellectually, then truly the experience has been more worth while, but basically and foremost the theatre must give its audience an emotional experience.

In exchange for the time given by the audience, it is the further obligation of the theatre to give that audience far more of life than it could have lived in the same period of time. It must accent the lessons and truths it presents and paint the characters so vividly that the audience may come to know and understand them. The story may parallel or may differ radically from life as experienced by the audience, but it must always furnish the vicarious experience and emotion that only the theatre can give.

Except for a very short period in the last century, man has always demanded that the theatre as an art must *seem* real rather than be real; that it must *reflect* life and not *be* life; that it be always an *illusion* of reality. It is in this element of *seeming* that we find the real art of the theatre, though the exact degree has varied throughout the ages and throughout the many types and forms of drama and theatre. Shakespeare's admonition: "Hold the mirror up to nature," supposes a special kind of mirror—one that pictures for the audience just what the artist would have it see, but in that seeing never confuses art with life itself.

A fourth obligation of the theatre is always to make the audience *believe* what it sees—at least for the time being. The light of the morrow and the process of careful analysis may show up some improbabilities of certain acts or characterizations, but these must never be obvious at the time. The emotion, spirit and illusion of life must be present.

Finally, the theatre must at all times tell the truth about its people and about life. When it lies or the audience no longer believes it, at that moment it ceases to exist as an art. This does not mean that plays must be realistic in their style and the settings naturalistic or even that the subject matter must be close to the actual. A fantasy can be just as true as the most realistic play if the characters

22

in that fantasy and the setting before which it is played *are consistent with the laws of their imagined existence. Alice in Wonderland* and *The Blue Bird* are just as true as the most realistic motion picture. Their truth or theme may be far more lasting in our memory.

To summarize, the theatre's five obligations to its audience are:

1. The theatre must make its appeal to the audience rather than to the individual.

2. The theatre must move its audience emotionally.

3. The theatre must give its audience more of life than they could live in the same period of time.

4. The theatre must *seem* real as it creates an illusion of life.

5. Theatrical illusion must be a truthful picture of life and one that the audience must believe—at least while in the theatre.

Likewise, the audience owes certain obligations to the theatre, for theatregoing is a two-way game. The *good* playgoer does not look upon the theatre as merely a temporary vacation from his own personal problems. He asks that it be more than mere escape, and he puts no limitations on the artist's conceptions or beliefs, but permits him to use whatever material he may need to tell his story. He does not demand any particular style of entertainment—other than that it be good theatre, whether it is the work of a clown, a *Hamlet*, a tragedy of Sophocles, or slapstick comedy. When he enters the theatre, he makes a certain surrender to it—not a blind surrender, for he retains his judgment and his taste. He accepts the theatre as make-believe, as a world built for him by many people, all participating in an effort to picture something of life by way of the artist's conception, and he, as part of the audience, will try to evaluate these efforts.

The good playgoer realizes that the theatre is a synthesis of all the arts and that many individuals are responsible for the production he is to witness. He does not think only in terms of the story, or the actors, or the scenery, or the lighting or the costumes. He realizes that he may like some part of the production and be disappointed in another; and that it is unjust to condemn or praise the whole because of some single contribution. He appreciates the fact that the theatre is capable of moving him in many ways; that it can stir, excite, amuse, teach, or transform, but that the whole experience is a two-way proposition—a game which he, too, must play.

He knows that at the very heart of all theatre pleasure is what Shakespeare called "imaginary puissance" or a sort of temporary half-belief. This half-belief does not demand that he blindly say: "That is Hamlet's castle," or "That is the home of Willy Loman," but that he does not set up in his mind the argument that it is *not* Elsinore or the home of Willy Loman. Coleridge once said: "True stage illusion consists not in the mind's judging it to be a forest, but in its remission of judgment that it is *not* a forest." Others have called this a suspension of disbelief.

The *poor* theatregoer is sometimes disturbed when he sees people he knows playing parts that are contrary to his accepted beliefs, as in the case of the college professor who said to the director: "Please don't ever cast one of our fine young people in an objectionable role, for always afterward one is reminded of that character when he meets him on the street," and the irate mother whose son was playing a part that required him to say: "Damn . . . Damn . . . Damn!" In either case the individuals were utterly lacking in any imaginary puissance. They refused to give each actor his right as an artist to be an actor and to speak the lines of someone else.

Contrary to this narrow and wholly unjustified viewpoint, the good playgoer gives the actors, the scenic artist and all those involved with the production the opportunity of taking him into their imaginary world. When these actors, these technicians, and this director have failed to accomplish their goal, after the playgoer has given them ample opportunity through his imaginary puissance, then he has the right to offer whatever adverse criticism of them as artists that he may desire. It will show more intelligence on his part, however, and give him greater personal pleasure if he is able to tell *why* they have or have not failed to accomplish their goals.

The good playgoer recognizes his own personal prejudices and tries to rise above them. He may not care for a given actor or for a particular type of dramatic event, but he does make an effort to judge each honestly by giving every artist his right to work as he chooses.

The final obligation of the audience—as well as the first—is a restatement of Principle 1, our basic premise of dramatic criticism: the three questions of Goethe.

In summary, it is the obligation of each member of the audience:

1. to view each dramatic event with an ample supply of imaginary puissance;

2. to recognize his own personal prejudices;

3. to observe and evaluate the work of *all* the artists who have made the production possible;

4. to give each artist the right to express himself as he desires;

5. to ask—always—the three questions of Goethe:

> *What is the artist trying to do?*
> *How well has he done it?*
> *Is it worth the doing?*

The reader will do well to understand these basic obligations, for they are the starting point in any critical analysis of a theatre experience. Each will receive almost constant consideration as we discuss the various theatre artists and their techniques in the chapters that follow.

Opinions

To complete the outline of this chapter we now point out some of our own opinions just as we have listed examples of facts and some of those principles which are fundamental to our own theory of dramatic criticism.

These statements are all opinions and have grown out of having accepted and applied the principles that have been discussed in addition to others that will be presented in the following chapters.

1. That television is not as bad as it is frequently pictured, and though it does not often attain the heights it is capable of reaching, it does have much to offer for those persons who possess "dialman-

ship" (which John Mason Brown defines as selectivity or self-editing), and that it may very well become the theatre of the future.

2. That the stage is more effective than either the motion pictures or television because of its aliveness, its immediacy, and its personal touch, and that there are few experiences more exciting than those that grow out of the excitement of playgoing—part of which is that proverbial shiver of anticipation one experiences when the house lights dim and the curtain is about to rise on a whole new world of imagination.

3. That *Our Town* by Thornton Wilder and *Death of a Salesman* by Arthur Miller are two of the greatest American plays yet written and that Eugene O'Neill is the greatest playwright our nation has yet produced.

4. That acting on the stage or in live television demands greater discipline and acting talent than that in motion pictures and that some of the finest acting performances the writer has witnessed have been Ethel Barrymore in *The Corn Is Green;* Helen Hayes in *Victoria Regina* and *Mary of Scotland;* Lynn Fontanne and Alfred Lunt in *There Shall Be No Night* and *The Visit;* Leslie Howard in *Hamlet;* John Gielgud in *The Importance of Being Earnest;* Tallulah Bankhead in *The Little Foxes.*

5. That the arena stage or any theatre production that spills over into the audience is less effective than those which follow the principles of illusion and emphasize a sharp distinction in the actor and audience relationship.

One can readily see that opinions are the easiest of the three sources of information with which we shall deal. Every man, woman or child who witnesses a dramatic performance is eager to express his opinion of that production. Some, of course, are better equipped than others to give an artistically honest evaluation. The opinions of experienced critics such as Brooks Atkinson of *The New York Times,* Walter Kerr of *The New York Herald-Tribune,* John Gassner of the Yale School of Drama, or Eric Bentley of *The New Republic* are always worthy of consideration, though as individuals we may

not agree with them. Nevertheless, thousands of playgoers await
their opinions after an opening before making plans to see the play.
In television, the critic and his opinion may have less power because what he has to say is not known until the event has been
completed. Some TV critics whose words are valued very highly,
however, are John Crosby of *The New York Herald Tribune* or Jack
Gould of *The New York Times.*

In the realm of the motion pictures the drama critic carries much
weight, for local critics review a picture soon after it has opened
and what is said may have a considerable bearing on the attendance.
This is equally true, on a national scale where the opinions of such
motion picture reviewers as Bosley Crowther of *The New York
Times,* John McCarter of *The New Yorker,* William Zinsser of *The
New York Herald Tribune* or many others may influence the attendance for any given motion picture. All these critics are considered
authorities in their respective fields and consequently their opinions
carry great power. They arrive at their opinions only after having
weighed and analyzed each individual performance in the scales of
their own principles and knowledge of the theatre and the previous
work of the artist. Each will have an adequate reason for whatever
decision he may have reached regarding the artistic merit of the
work he has seen. He may not seem to give much thought to an
underlying principle out of which his decision has grown, for that
principle has now become part of his background. It is the sub-
strata of his critical analysis—taste—dramatic understanding—
appreciation—ability to judge. He now works as does the experienced athlete who moves with smoothness, grace and precision
without giving his body a thought, or as your grandmother does
who prepares her famous three-layer cake without any apparent
guidance. At one time the critic—the athlete—or your grandmother
was most conscious of the principles, the order and care with which
each bodily movement was made, or the exact measurement of each
ingredient.

In like manner, you may not remember the minute details of

27

these pages, but the essence of what they say can become a part of that background and sense of theatre we included earlier as a requisite for any good dramatic critic.

Finally, we would emphasize that a unanimity of opinion regarding any performance is neither possible nor probable. Agreement or objectivity where emotion is concerned is not expected. Even with the same set of principles (which is improbable) two persons will arrive at a widely different opinion regarding the work of any artist in the theatre. This is due to many reasons—a few of which are never consciously sensed—emotions, personal appeal, and interests —the very nature of the individual.

What we do hope to do is increase the enjoyment of the theatre for a few of those millions who have suddenly had the drama become a part of their daily lives and who know very little about it. We believe that real enjoyment comes only after the desire for escape and entertainment has been fulfilled and also that real enjoyment involves knowing why our attention has or has not been held.

It is our conviction that we, the audience, cannot answer Goethe's three questions until we have recognized the distinction between the substance, form, and technique of each theatre artist. We must know where each begins and ends; we must have some familiarity with the principles of form that have been established over many hundreds of years, and we must come to appreciate the artist's personal technique, originality and imagination which have helped him to blend the substance and form of his art and to bring forth something that is peculiarly his own work.

The play and the playwright

THE PLAY: DEFINITION—TOOLS OF THE PLAYWRIGHT—
HIS SUBSTANCE

Literally, the written manuscript of the play is a drama. In the theatre it is referred to as "the script." It does not actually become a play until it is brought to life by actors and before an audience. The very spelling of the word—*playwright*—rather than *playwrite* would indicate that a play is *made* rather than *written*—made by the contributing efforts of all those individuals who are responsible for the full production. The written drama is only the seed out of which has grown the play—a most complex organism with an identity all its own. As a play the written script becomes a new work of art involving the *interpretation* of the playwright's creation on the part of the actors, the scene designer, the costumer and other technicians. All these artists are more than mere interpreters, for they, too, are creating as the written drama becomes something new so far as form is concerned. It is the director who, in our modern theatre, unifies and pulls together all their varied efforts and so translates the drama into a play. Even that organism will vary from performance to performance by the reaction of the audience, and in this book we are always thinking in terms of the total play rather than the written drama as such.

In our opening chapter we said that a play is a movement toward

HOW WELL HAS HE ACCOMPLISHED IT? ⟶

WHAT IS THE PLAYWRIGHT TRYING TO DO?

⟶ WAS IT WORTH THE DOING?

THE PLAYWRIGHT'S SUBSTANCE

What is the story he is
trying to tell?—The theme
he is trying to proclaim? What
is he trying to say to us, to
make us feel or understand?

His Tools

plot, theme, mood,
characters, dialogue,
spectacle.

THE PLAYWRIGHT'S FORM

The type of play he
has chosen;
the aesthetic style
he has used to
suggest or imitate
life;
the structure of his
play.

THE PLAYWRIGHT'S TECHNIQUE

His blending of theme
and plot;
his personal style;
his treatment of
material;
his strategy and
tactics;
theatrical or
literary;
tests of greatness.

30

something. Many years ago someone quite aptly defined a play as a trap in which the characters were either falling into an inevitable situation or struggling to get out of one. We would choose as a more complete definition the one that Clayton Hamilton has given us: *A play is a story devised to be presented by actors on a stage before an audience.* The play—on paper—is only an expression of a mood, the painting of a personality, the telling of a story, the projection of a theme or truth as the dramatist sees and feels it—in short, an imitation or a reflection of some selected segment of life. Unlike the novelist, the poet, or the essayist, the playwright must constantly think in terms of how the words will sound to the ear rather than how they look on the printed page. He must omit descriptions and speak in terms of action and movement. He must constantly be aware of the pictorial effect, the rhythm of speech, the setting, the properties, and the acting. He must know the limitations of the physical theatre and realize that the theatregoer can not go back and check a speech or re-read it to make sure he has got the full meaning. The characters he creates must be vital and interesting individuals with dynamic personalities. Not many of our acquaintances will fit into a play. There, every individual must be distinctive, possessing both a will and a purpose. In real life we are often unsure of the motives behind the actions of our fellow human beings, but in a play we must be sure or the characters become blurred. There must be a conflict or at least some element of crisis in the action. Something must constantly be happening, and this must be revealed through the acts or lines rather than by exposition on the part of the author or by speeches of the other actors. A play must possess dramatic movement which means something is happening to the characters through reaction. There must always be growth or change of some kind. It need not be physical, but a constant alteration of relationships must always be present.

The playwright must think in terms of the physical theatre of his day, and that structure determines both the form and the aesthetic style of his play. Historically, that physical theatre has been responsible for the majestic beauty of the Greeks who wrote for huge outdoor religious spectacles, the poetic power of the Elizabethans, the brilliant and often vulgar theatre of the Restoration, the artificial and extreme morality of the Victorians, and, finally, the language spoken by the men in the streets or by our next-door neighbor in the more realistic theatre that came into prominence soon after the middle of the last century.

A playwright frequently writes with specific actors in mind whom he knows will be able to portray his roles. Our best evidence that Richard Burbage must have been a great actor is that William Shakespeare wrote for him such roles as Hamlet, Macbeth, King Lear, and others. Many plays have appeared great in the hands of the actor for whom they were written and have lost that prestige when he was no longer able to play the role.

More than any other man in literature, the playwright must write with an audience rather than the individual in mind. He knows that one audience will vary from another in nature, education, or background, and from country to country. Other literary men may create for a small group or class or even the individual. They may choose their clientele—but not the writer of a play. He must appeal to every member of his audience from the youngest child and most uneducated adult to the oldest citizen or deepest thinker of his day. A poet may compose his work so that it is understood or appreciated only by the most brilliant mind, but for the playwright to do so would be suicide. A full appreciation of any play is dependent upon a knowledge of the relation of the subject to the time and society for which it was written.

The tools of the playwright are the very elements of drama. They include the story or plot (the specific incidents that make up the story), the theme or idea (which is the truth or generalization concerning life that the play is trying to make), the characters that are involved, the language or dialogue they speak, and the mood or atmosphere that the play would create. A sixth element enters when the work is not sufficiently endowed with story, theme, character, mood, or language to hold an audience. This element is frequently called spectacle and rarely possesses any real literary value. It may be found in the use of mob scenes, beautiful costumes, musical backgrounds, dance extravaganzas, sequences that present elaborate stage pictures but make little contribution to the ultimate goal. Spectacle is resorted to only in a last effort to get or hold the interest of an audience. The frequent use of spectacle in the motion picture and television is the most common criticism of these mediums.

The playwright's substance is basically what he is trying to tell as a story, to develop by way of a mood or a well-drawn character or to propound as a theme or basic truth of life.

FORM IN PLAYWRITING

Type of play

The drama elements that dominate the play will largely determine the type of play it is to be. If the material is of a serious nature, it will be either a tragedy or a melodrama; if it is to be treated in a lighter vein, even though the subject itself is a serious one, it may be a comedy or a farce.

The very "requirements" that are here listed for each of the four types are arbitrary and may change with the years. Though they may even now be debated, they have been derived from what is generally considered as the best of our dramatic literature in the various types.

TRAGEDY

Tragedy is the oldest written drama. It has always been of a very serious nature and is ranked as one of the most artistic works of civilized man. Its story has always presented the spectacle of a great or noble human being shattering himself against insuperable obstacles because he will not compromise with circumstances or conditions as they exist. The Greeks were in conflict with the gods, the Elizabethans with some fault within themselves, and the moderns have found their conflict in their surroundings, but always the force is greater than the individual and he must go down in defeat. The leading character, or the protagonist as he is called, has until recent times been a person of high station or an individual with some nobility. In more modern plays he has been a representative of a class or a social group.

Two specific emotions experienced by an audience in great tragedy are pity and fear—pity for the hero who seems to be suffering unjustly, and fear that the same circumstances could apply to us.

The most essential factor in great tragedy is what the Greek philosopher Aristotle called *catharsis* or an emotional cleansing. Modern translators have called this a purification or purgation of the emotions. In the area of psychoanalysis it is the elimination of complexes and frustrations by bringing them into consciousness and affording them expression. The leading figure on the stage passes through a great crisis and in that crisis comes to realize a personal weakness or fault within himself. He may have lost the battle and his life—but he dies a happier and better man for having recognized that error.

John Gassner, one of our finest modern critics, has called this recognition *enlightenment.* By this he does not mean the gaining of some knowledge through the lines of the play or the coming of any information that may alter the course of the plot. It is nothing in the action or dialogue, but something felt or achieved by the leading character and through him transferred to the audience. Mr. Gassner says that pity, fear, and enlightenment thus become a "marriage of emotion and understanding." This feeling must rise above the perturbing events of the play.

We in the audience, with full knowledge of our own frustrations, inhibitions, personal faults and weaknesses, see those human errors brought out into the open on the stage, and thus we, too, are spiritually cleansed. It serves as a sort of public confession, but this is not enough in itself. We must put our own houses in order by resolving to go out of the theatre better men or women and to cast these evil elements out of our being.

It is this enlightenment that is so essential to tragedy. Sometimes it happens in the audience and sometimes it is only sensed or recognized by the audience as it occurs within the leading character in the play. It is our own recognition or failure to recognize this enlightenment that causes so much debate over whether much of our modern serious drama is tragedy or melodrama. So much depends on our own background, knowledge, and sensitivity.

In modern literature we have very few tragedies. There are some that lie, as Mr. Gassner says, "in the foothills," but few that can stand beside *Hamlet, Oedipus the King, Electra, Macbeth, King Lear,* and other famous literary masterpieces. *Death of a Salesman, Long Day's Journey Into Night, Winterset, The House of Bernalda Alba, Desire Under the Elms,* and *Blood Wedding* are a few modern plays that have created much discussion as to whether or not they have reached the heights of tragedy.

Rarely on the screen have we seen great tragedy. There the temptation to bring in the effects of chance, excitement, and sentimentality have changed the possibility of tragedy into melodrama— frequently of a high order—but melodrama nevertheless.

If we study the tragedies from all periods, we find there are at least five basic principles. When a playwright fails to meet *any one* of these demands, his drama is pushed outside the realm of pure tragedy.

REQUIREMENTS OF TRAGEDY

1. The play must concern a serious subject.
2. The leading character must be a great figure or one that is representative of a class. He must represent more than an individual.
3. The incidents must be absolutely honest and without the element of coincidence or chance. What should happen must happen.
4. The basic emotions are those of pity and fear—pity for the protagonist in his suffering, and fear that the same fate might come to us.
5. In the final analysis the protagonist must meet defeat, but before that defeat must come enlightenment or the *catharsis* of Aristotle.

MELODRAMA

Where the tragic writer says: "What is the one thing these people would do under these circumstances?" the writer of melodrama says: "What is the most thrilling action I can devise here?" and then: "How can I make it seem logical that the characters would do this?" This often brings about inconsistent characterizations of those involved in the plot. One escapade rapidly follows another, and the excitement that ensues makes it one of the most entertaining and popular types of drama. More than 90 per cent of the serious motion pictures or television plays we see are melodramas, and yet many are so well disguised that a majority of those who see and praise them would be indignant if we suggested that they had seen a melodrama.

Webster defines melodrama as "a kind of drama, commonly romantic and sensational, with both songs and instrumental music interspersed; hence, any romantic and sensational drama, typically with a happy ending." The name grew out of the expression, *drama with music,* for melodrama had its origin under those circumstances. The stage later abandoned the music. The motion pictures readopted it as part of their own technique, and as one sees the motion picture melodrama today with the almost inevitable musical background, he wonders if the cycle may not have completed itself.

Perhaps a word in defense would not be out of place, for the term melodrama unfortunately is very much in disrepute. This has grown out of those melodramas which came to us in the late nineteenth century, such as *Bertha, the Sewing-Machine Girl; The Streets of New York; Ten Nights in a Barroom; East Lynne,* and hundreds of others. In these plays black was black and white was white. The playwright pitted good against evil, excitement was the key word, and coincidence a commonplace. Because of its connotation many persons feel that to praise a melodrama or to admit a liking for it is a mark of discredit, without realizing that the vast majority of serious plays written since 1900 fall naturally into this type. Both tragedy and melodrama are legitimate methods for planning a serious play, for by either it is possible to give a truthful representation of life. Life itself is divided between chance and character. Melodrama would make more of the chance; tragedy would place emphasis upon character. Melodrama would show what might happen; tragedy would show what must happen. While tragedy must *tell the truth,* melodrama *must not lie,* and the world knows full well there is a vast difference between those two injunctions! Arthur Miller has said: "When I show you why a man does what he does, I may do it melodramatically; but when I show you why he almost did not do it, I am making drama." In melodrama there is a chance of victory, for the protagonist is the victim of external circumstances over which he may win; tragedy exists when the protagonist *has within him the power to win,* but is, nevertheless, doomed to failure.

Within the last ten years we have been given many excellent melodramas, both on the stage and on the screen. Although the element of chance may enter, the plays do not lie. The characters are involved in the most exciting events that can be conceived, and the leading character may emerge from one situation only to be plunged immediately into another. The whole play is episodic. While the basic emotion may be pity, the element of sentimentality is always present. Sentimentality is said to exist when we are so anxious to experience an emotion vicariously that we do not pause to discriminate just so long as we get the thrill. We sympathize with a child because he is a child or with a pretty girl just because she is pretty and in distress without analyzing the causes. In reality, neither may really deserve our sympathy. Sentimentality—by this definition—is said to exist when we are permitted to experience an emotion without paying for it, for the sentimentalist lives on wishful thinking, on emotion rather than reason. He sees just what he wants to see. To him life is a conflict between good and bad—with no inbetween. He refuses to apply intelligence and fact to a situation or to think it through. Instead he relies solely on human feeling. Favorite stories show the young man struggling to be honest against the commercially-minded world; the innocence of childhood; downtrodden minority groups; the successful struggles of poor but honest persons; motherhood; the rehabilitation of gamblers, gangsters, women of the streets and drunkards; and the complete revival of the hard-hearted and stingy old man whose soul is saved through the love of a little child. Sentimentality is an important segment of of melodrama. There may be fear, but it is of a more temporary or surface variety. We are most interested in the situation and the circumstances than we are in the intricacies of the characters involved. Sentimentality under control can possess great emotional power; out of control it only lies.

The characters in melodrama being as unauthentic as they are, the members of the audience are able to fit themselves into any role and thus receive a greater vicarious enjoyment. The story seems to deal with charmed lives, for the ending is nearly always a happy one. Herein lies the greatest appeal of melodrama to the average motion picture, television, or theatre audience. It furnishes them an excitement and a happiness often denied them in their everyday existence, for more often than not the protagonist wins his struggle. In melodrama there is never the enlightenment as we envision it.

As in tragedy, there are five comparable principles which can be considered as basic in the study of any melodrama:

REQUIREMENTS OF MELODRAMA

1. It treats of a serious subject.
2. The characters are more loosely drawn than in tragedy, and this makes it easier for the audience to identify itself with the characters, thus creating a stronger empathic response.
3. Whereas tragedy must be absolutely honest, the element of chance enters into the melodrama. It is episodic and the most exciting incidents possible are brought into the play.
4. There may be an emotion of pity, but it borders on sentimentality. Fear may be evident, but it is of a more temporary or surface type.
5. There is no real enlightenment even in defeat, and in most instances the protagonist does win his battle.

One can always justify a good melodrama, both as escape and as an artistic theatrical experience. As escape it receives its greatest popularity with the masses, because it permits them to forget their own troubles; although they may view the troubles of someone else, the experience is a vicarious one. There is no strain or suffering on their part. These are the basic reasons for the preponderance of melodramas on our TV and motion picture screens.

As critics we should evaluate each type in its own realm of theatrical entertainment, for each should be accepted as a wholly legitimate means of relating a serious story.

THE AREAS OF COMEDY

Man is the only animal capable of realizing the miseries of life, and he is the only one who has been given the privilege of knowing how to laugh at those miseries. He likes to make the most of that opportunity, and psychologists have tried to find the reason for his laughter since psychology became a science. The elements or areas of comedy have been given us by Alan Reynolds Thompson.* His "ladder of comedy" is our clearest picturization of this subject. If studied carefully it can be most helpful in differentiation between the two types of humor—comedy and farce. The reader must never forget, however, that the artist's treatment or presentation of the material will determine whether it is high farce which borders on comedy or low comedy which borders on farce. This does not imply that one is any better than the other. Each is a legitimate method of presenting a lighter story.

Farce   *High Comedy*

6. Comedy of ideas and satire

5. Inconsistencies of character

4. Verbal wit

3. Plot devices

2. Physical mishaps

1. Obscenity

Obscenity is considered the lowest form of comedy. It needs little explanation and is very scarce in our own modern theatre, except when combined with one of the higher forms of humor as a necessary part of a specific character or situation. There have been times in dramatic literature when the digestive processes or the most animalistic elements of love-making were wholly acceptable on the

---

* Alan Reynolds Thompson, *The Anatomy of the Drama* (Berkeley: University of California Press, 1946).

stage. The audience expected and accepted these as a logical part of the play.

The repartee of the upper classes during the Restoration would be highly shocking to even the most sophisticated audience of the twentieth century. One wonders as he reads some of these dramas how they could ever have been put on the stage. They are frequently so edited in a modern American production that it is little wonder they lose much of the humor we know they had in their day. These same plays, however, in the hands of an English cast, familiar with the style of writing and capable of catching that style in their playing can make the plays not only hilariously funny, but in doing so, they eliminate any shade of obscenity we find in the reading or detect when handled by less understanding actors.

In recent times New York has accepted and praised plays which many of our non-commercial theatres would not dare attempt, not necessarily because the material was obscene, but because they as actors or producers would be incapable of treating it as well as it had been done by the playwright and trained artists of the professional theatre.

Moving up the ladder of comedy, we come to *physical mishap*. This, too, is exactly what it says. The most obvious is the common "pratt-fall" such as having a chair jerked out from under an unsuspecting character, or a banana peel that sends someone sprawling across the stage, the custard pie thrown in the face, the dignified man or woman caught in the stream of water from a hose. Much of what is called slapstick comedy comes in this category. These physical eventualities are found today only in the broadest of comedy, or in an occasional motion picture or TV farce. When they do appear, the discerning critic cannot refrain from exclaiming, "Oh, no, no, not that, please!", for the distinction is so fine between farce which we must believe and burlesque which we need not believe, that it takes a real artist to know and to keep within these boundaries.

The third step is *plot device*. Shakespeare, whose comedies have

40

never been considered on a par with his tragedies, has often turned to this type of comedy but has done it most effectively. It involves misunderstandings, cross purposes, inopportune or embarrassing occurrences, mistaken identity, and so on. In this area of comedy the author manipulates the characters and situations into the most hilarious combinations and ludicrous situations.

The next step is *verbal wit*. Even in reading, this dialogue will seem humorous and as a play will send an audience into gales of laughter the first time it is heard. In the English language few playwrights have surpassed Oscar Wilde and his great gift at this sort of comedy. He is known for such epigrams as: "To love oneself is the beginning of a lifelong romance"; "Wicked women bother one. Good women bore one. That is the only difference between them"; "There's nothing in the world like the devotion of a married woman. It's a thing no married man knows anything about"; "Experience is the name everybody gives to their mistakes"; and one as modern as "Spies are of no use nowadays. The newspapers do their work instead." His *The Importance of Being Earnest* is considered our most perfect example of verbal wit.

In America George Kaufman, Moss Hart, and S. N. Behrman are known for their wit in such plays as *The Man Who Came to Dinner, You Can't Take It With You, First Lady,* and others. Like Wilde they, too, occasionally give treatment to the characters who will speak the lines so that the distinction between farce and comedy is difficult to make.

These four elements of comedy—obscenity, physical eventualities, plot device, and verbal wit—are considered the basic materials of farce. The fact that they are ranked low on the ladder of comedy does not mean that they should be considered any the less artistic. In most of the examples that have been given, the authors have been able *by their treatment* to lift the farcical material to a high degree of artistry as farce which is always a legitimate part of comedy. We could point out many plays that have failed because the same material had received inadequate treatment, and the plays were for that reason undistinguished. It is very important that we be able to recognize the material itself and also the treatment it has received by the artist. These are separate entities.

Character is the foundation of comedy, and *inconsistency of character* is our next step in the ladder of comedy. It consists of the unexpected on the part of an individual; the surprise action or speech so contrary to his appearance or nature and yet believable as a characteristic rather than for the sake of a humorous touch only.

In the theatre, as in life, man has attained the pinnacle of humor when he reaches what Mr. Thompson has called a *comedy of ideas* or *satire*. These qualities of humor are found in man's ability to laugh at that which is closest to his heart—his family, his friends, his religion, his politics, his country, himself. It is a gift of irreverence—an ability to kid the things we take seriously. One is said to have a real sense of humor when he can appreciate the humor of his own pretensions and short-comings. This is sometimes called high comedy and may be defined as a criticism of life, though we must point out that farce, too, by its treatment is often raised to the level of satire. Sometimes the laughter may be violent and angry, and again delightful, tongue-in-cheek, accompanied by an intensity of purpose because the characters involved, and we as an audience, realize the seriousness of their acts and thoughts as well as the humor involved in them.

The very proximity of farce to comedy in the realm of humor is exemplified by the common denominator of the highest comedy and the lowest farcical material in that they both demand a sense of detachment on the part of the audience. Both frown upon sentiment or sentimentality, and neither will tolerate the audience identifying itself with what it sees on the stage. Both high comedy and farce regard life objectively, and either can be a strong agent toward eliminating social injustice or the individual's deflections in his own personal habits. As Molière has wisely said: "People do not mind being wicked, but they object to being made ridiculous."

We would emphasize once more that even though Mr. Thompson's ladder indicates farce and comedy materials as belonging to different levels, the highest of comedy could be made to appear the lowest of farce, or the most blatant farce could by its treatment be lifted into the realm of comedy. This is by way of saying that nothing in itself must be either one or the other, but that the treatment of the artists may make the material one or the other.

The diagram and discussion will bear careful study and analysis, for if they are understood by the reader, they can be of great assistance in his effort to distinguish between comedy and farce.

Comedy is the most miscellaneous of all the dramatic forms and therefore the most difficult to define. There are some who, when in doubt, measure a given play as tragedy, melodrama or farce, and when it has failed to meet any of these requirements, call it comedy. We know that it must present believable and understandable characters; that the situations should be both possible and probable; that it treat of the individual and his personal problems; and that it concern the lighter side of life. While a comedy may often use a serious subject as its substance, such as infidelity, war, communism, tolerance, religion, marriage, or divorce, it does treat that subject more lightly than in tragedy or melodrama. In comedy, as in tragedy, the protagonist has within him the power to alter the immediate obstacle in his way.

Much of comedy is based on incidents occurring in the life of others which provoke laughter in us, but if these same incidents were happening to us, we would find them unpleasant. In this special brand of comedy it is the element of perspective that gives us the detachment we need. The seriousness with which the characters involved attack the problem provokes us to laughter. This is exemplified by the cartoon of the father leading his small son toward the woodshed and carrying a paddle in one hand. The caption reads: "Dad, you know we're both going to laugh at this about thirty years from now." Perspective is a vital factor in comedy.

In comedy the protagonist usually overcomes his obstacles, but the means of his success should be consistent with the laws of life.

We may, as an audience, laugh at the situations even while we sympathize with the characters. A common and mistaken belief is that comedies must have a happy ending. The conclusion must be honest in the spirit of the play, but need not be a happy one.

Historically, the Greeks revelled in a rollicking sort of humor with much biting satire. The Romans leaned toward buffoonery and ingenious plots. The Elizabethans gave us the romantic comedy of Shakespeare with its lyrical poetry and light-hearted stories of love and adventure. In addition there was the comedy of Ben Jonson with bitter satire and ridicule of the man in the street.

Molière is considered to be the greatest writer of comedy that has ever lived. His was the most skillful satire, and his plays are said to have evoked the "thoughtful laughter" which is the final and true test of comedy. This is in contrast with the "thoughtless laughter" brought forth by the farcical elements described in the following section. Various names have been given this phase of comedy, such as *comedy of manners, high comedy, artificial comedy,* and *intellectual comedy,* but the purpose is to satirize the social customs of the upper classes. It creates thoughtful laughter, though it may not stir our emotions very deeply. Sheldon Cheney has said:

> True comedy arises rather out of character, usually the clash of foibles in character against common-sense truth; out of the vices and weaknesses of human nature held up to ridicule. If at the same time sympathy is aroused, the play borders on sentimental comedy. What is generally accepted as essential comedy, "high" comedy, is the satiric sort, untinged with sympathetic appeal.*

No one would question that comedy is one of the most popular of all types, being challenged only by farce. If man wants escape he can usually find it through laughter, and too often he cares not how it is provoked.

This brief description of what comedies have been and do include, plus the differentiation which preceded, should now make it possible to draw up some basic tests for comedy.

* Sheldon Cheney, *The Theatre* (New York: Longmans, Green & Co., 1930).

THE REQUIREMENTS OF COMEDY

A survey of the best comedies in twenty-five hundred years of theatre shows that comedy:

1. treats its subject in a lighter vein even though the subject may be a serious one;
2. provokes what can be defined as "thoughtful laughter";
3. is both possible and probable;
4. grows out of character rather than situation;
5. is honest in its portrayal of life.

FARCE

A common error is to use the word *comedy* while thinking in terms of farce. Farce is to comedy what melodrama is to tragedy. It consists of exaggerated incidents and characters with a domination of plot and only a pretense of reality. More often than not it develops on a series of misunderstandings between the characters involved. The generalization is still good that comedy is both possible and probable, while farce is possible, but not very probable. Farce has been called a purely mathematical sequence of laughs. The object of the author is to make the audience believe only for the moment. The incidents come rapidly, and the whole play is episodic. The audience is given little time to think because farce portrays the strictly ludicrous in life; if the spectators did analyze the action, believability would be sacrificed. Farce depends upon extreme improbability which usually grows out of someone's mental or physical distress. It is a paradox that this type of humor has always flourished most in ages of great cultural activity and refinement. The reason lies in the fact that farce, though improbable, is usually based on logic and objectivity, qualities which are an integral part of education and culture.

The author of a farce usually asks the audience to grant him a few improbabilities at the very beginning, but from this point on, he proceeds in a world of reality. It is often true that a farce exists when the whole story would evaporate and the play be concluded if at any time each character of the story were to tell the whole truth. However, it is our acceptance of this opening improbability or this lack of common knowledge to all the characters that makes the series of events so highly enjoyable.

While observing a farce in production we should, with a modicum of imaginary puissance, believe what we are watching. We may not believe the story or the characters once out of the theatre, and perhaps not even during the intermissions, but while the actual performance is on, there must be a sense of believability—at least in a detached, fairy-story degree.

One of our most famous farces is *Charley's Aunt* which Ray Bolger made into the very popular musical comedy, *Where's Charley*. As a popular stage piece this has had one of the most amazing careers. Ludicrous as it is in content, an audience is ready to accept the improbabilities and howl with laughter with temporary belief—*if* the players attack these improbable situations with sincerity—because it is so theatrically effective. Measured by the tests which follow, this play becomes an almost perfect example of farce.

The dialogue of farce may run from the epigram of Oscar Wilde to the "gag" in the most recent radio or television script. In either instance any speech could be given to almost any character in the play, for the lines have no special relationship to character but exist for the laugh value they may possess. We can see the logic of this fact when we realize that the term *farce* comes to us from the Latin word meaning "to stuff."

Like melodrama, farce is most delightful when done well. The motion pictures lean heavily to this type and in it have done some of their most superior work. Some years ago there was an influx of English farces, notably those of Alec Guinness, which added much to our appreciation of their value.

The Requirements of Farce

The qualities of farce which have been most constant through the ages show that it:

1. has as its object riotous laughter and escape;

2. asks the audience to accept certain improbabilities, but from that point proceeds in a life-like manner;

3. is possible, but not very probable;

4. is dominated by situation rather than character, and calls for little or no thought;

5. must move very rapidly in an episodic manner, and is believable only for the moment.

Aesthetic style

A second factor in the playwright's form is that of aesthetic style. The most common aesthetic styles are the classic which grew out of the open-air Greek theatres; the romantic, of which Shakespeare is considered the greatest contributor, at least in the English-speaking world; and the realistic with which we are most familiar in our modern theatre. Less used, but important, are symbolism, which is sometimes found mixed with any of the other styles, and expressionism which has been used in an effort to break away from the ultra realistic. Fantasy is frequently considered a style in itself. This is a fairy-tale quality highly imaginative and concerned with events and characters far from reality, but wholly true in that imagined world.

Once the dramatist begins to tell his story, he finds that he is either suggesting life as in the classic, romantic, or fantastic styles, or he is imitating life as in the realistic, and occasionally in the expressionistic. A frequent criticism of the untutored is that any play not using the language or style of speech with which we are all so familiar is "unnatural" or "unreal." This criticism, of course, rises from a basic misunderstanding of the words *reality* and *realism*. Reality is life itself; realism is the term used to denote the artist's aesthetic style in portraying that reality. Realism is reality reflected through the artist's personality and indicates selection and treatment given life by that artist in his imitation or suggestion of it. In the more imaginative world of the Greek theatre, of Shakespeare, or of the writers of fantasy, the characters are just as real and just as natural but in terms of the theatre and by suggestion. They are characters of a fictional reality and as such are more likely to live for future generations than are the so-called realistic characters of much of our modern drama. Hamlet, Macbeth, Romeo, Oedipus, Antigone, or Electra are less likely to become dated than are the characters in last night's TV production or the most recent Broadway success.

In the classic style there is a certain worship of form and orderliness. Choruses usually give us the necessary information or background; the language is often in verse; one mood predominates; comedy is not found next to tragedy in the same play, and there is a loftiness, dignity and distance on the part of the characters involved.

The romantic style is more indifferent to form and order. It disregards tradition and scorns the practical everyday life. Time may be telescoped; all is on a plane of imaginative grandeur. The idealistic or imaginative side of man is always present. The characters live what seem to be charmed lives in a world of theatre rather than a world of reality. Existence is filled with excitement, suspense, success. The locale is some faraway or fictitious place; the playwright is unhampered in placing his action or in the choice of characters. He may choose prose, or verse or silence, but he writes with a freedom, a beauty of language and an imagination that permits his characters to do and feel as we would like to think were possible.

Realism is an effort to picture reality as we know it, though it does select, arrange and discard as art must do. It stresses the practical everyday details of our existence and pictures the ugliness as well as the beauty. Man's most intimate problems are discussed, and the characters are those we might meet in our everyday lives. Time is all accounted for. An individual character's motives and actions must meet the tests of modern psychology. This is the style that was introduced by Henrik Ibsen, and it has dominated our theatre for almost one hundred years. It found its greatest forte in the motion pictures and even more so in television productions.

Expressionism is a recent aesthetic style and appeared first as a reaction against realism. It is more abstract and attempts to picture the character's impression through some distortion mentally or physically. There is a strong emphasis on mood. Scenes do not always follow in chronological order. The material becomes increasingly imaginative and sometimes even grotesque in picturing thought or inner feelings. *Death of a Salesman* was a happy combination of the realistic and the expressionistic styles as stark realism was pictured in one scene and the thoughts that existed in the mind of Willy Loman were enacted almost simultaneously with that realism. The screen gives great opportunity to expressionism but has not used it as extensively as it might.

Symbolism and fantasy are two further aesthetic styles. The first tells two stories at once in that one action is symbolic of another by calling to our mind another story. Fantasy is thoroughly imaginative, fairy-story-like, and embodies purely hypothetical situations. Most of Walt Disney is in the realm of fantasy. An occasional motion picture is in this style and many television scripts have used it successfully.

An effect of reality may be found in any aesthetic style. Fantasy —romanticism—classicism—may seem just as real as the most blatant realism. It is only necessary that the characters live and speak in the reality of their imagined world; that the playwright be consistent with the aesthetic style he has selected, whether he is suggesting or imitating life. There are many who would prefer the realistic style. No doubt the average man finds it easier to empathize with the characters in a realistic piece, for what they do comes closer to his own experience. Someone once said: "We must pay for what we get and we always get just what we pay for." What we have paid for our realism has been an over-all littleness of conception, language, and character.

Television was still in its infancy when it became evident that its major problem was material, and that the writer should be the most sought after individual in the whole of its personnel. Not only did this infant devour new scripts faster than they could be supplied, but it also consumed the dramatic literature of the past at an alarming rate. Although the television playwright is not necessarily doomed to realism, he has thus far found it to be his most fruitful field. The drama here must be more penetrating than either stage or cinema. The camera permits a delicacy and a subtleness that is impossible on the stage. Although it can be duplicated on the motion picture screen, both realism and detail excel in television more than in either of the other fields. On the stage there is only the semblance of realism. In the cinema the very size of the screen and the presence of the audience are handicaps. The great secret of television is to find one specific emotional moment or one facet of a character and to portray that so vividly that it will touch the same spring in the mind of the viewer. In real life the man next door or the completely normal person has little to offer dramatically. However, under the microscopic eye of the camera small details of character can be exposed that will make him a most interesting figure on the television screen.

The purpose of all mediums has been to present the normal and natural, especially in the realistic theatre. Here the motion picture screen and even more so the stage have worked under the most abnormal and unnatural situations. Now, in the privacy of home and the intimacy of the camera's close-up we can seek out the most realistic and exact emotion or feeling that has ever been known. Indeed, if it is realism we want, it is better portrayed on the television screen than at any time in all our history. No better medium exists for the portrayal of personal drama and inner feelings. This ability to speak so realistically to an audience steeped in realism is unquestionably one of the major reasons for its great popularity.

Structure

The third aspect of the playwright's form is the structure or building of his play. There are certain specific materials that every play must possess. They are generally called the exposition, the inciting moment, the rising action, the turning point, the falling action, the climax, and the conclusion. Each has its place in the structure of a play. The exposition usually is found in the first few minutes of the play, for this is where we learn who these characters are, what has happened before we met them, what they plan to do, their relationship or feelings toward each other—in short, the *status quo* of their world. Suddenly something occurs that upsets the apple-cart, that disturbs the picture or their world as we have found it. This something new that enters is called the inciting moment, and when it occurs we know at once what the play is going to be about—what the conflict is—what the characters are trying to get out of—what the actors want to bring into reality. The rising action is the next phase of the play in which we see the various forces in conflict, each striving for its own end. This continues until one force seems suddenly to get the advantage over the other, and that moment or situation is called the turning point. The falling action (which is a misnomer, for the interest of the audience must not fall) continues to build the intensity as some new factor enters the picture, and this added element brings about the climax which is the final culmination of everything that has been said or done by the characters during the production. The climax pulls all the threads together, for the whole play must have built to this moment. It is the solution of whatever conflict may have existed. Finally, there is the conclusion which establishes once more, at least for the moment, a *status quo* so that we may leave the theatre with some feeling that this situation, at least, has run its course or been resolved.

A *well-made* play (which is generally a derogatory term) is the play that follows this strategy exactly. In such a play we are able to foresee the whole story very soon after it has started. If this is possible the playwright has fallen down in his form, as well as in his technique, and it is frequently called *hack writing*. Sometimes exposition is stretched through the entire play, and it is possible for the turning point and climax to be almost the same; but every play must—soon after the curtain goes up—have something occur which sets the dramatic action in motion, an incident which is called the inciting moment, just as every play must build logically to some single most exciting and tense moment which is the climax.

It is often said that in a three-act play the first act is given to establishing a situation, the second to complicating it, and the third to resolving it. Few plays are that simple, but it is a fairly good over-all rule. A common criticism of television writers is that, because of their time limit, they leave out the third act. The setting up of a situation and its complication are the easiest parts to write. Resolving a story takes more time, more thought, and greater artistry. The necessity of rushing TV scripts into production is no doubt responsible for this justifiable criticism.

In its art of telling a story the motion picture resembles the novel far more than it does the drama, although the structure of the story itself does follow the pattern of a play. The motion picture need pay no attention to temporal order or the normal sequence of events. It can show anything that can be photographed and is at its best in pageants, huge sagas, spectacles, historical events, and so on.

One of the first laws of the screen is that there must be constant change and visual alteration. It is far easier to dramatize a novel for the screen than a play, for in the latter, it is not only necessary to reduce the dialogue, but to add many scenes which actually show what on the stage may be only discussed or related. Because the scene must constantly be changing, the motion picture cannot pause long enough to allow the significance beneath the surface to sink into the mind of the audience. Rarely does it turn inward to man's thoughts and do it effectively. The projection of subtle characterization or psychological aspects of character are extremely difficult. These are left for the better stage presentations. Characters far too often prove to be merely types rather than the individuals sought in the theatre.

Often a great stage success is made into a powerful film, but one only needs to have seen both productions to sense that this very important emphasis on subtlety of characterization, evident on the stage, has been lost in the motion picture.

TECHNIQUE IN PLAYWRITING

Theme and plot

The plot has been called the body of a play and the theme has been called its soul. Most plays have a conflict of some kind which may be between individuals, between man and society, man and some superior force, or man and himself. This conflict is the plot. One of the first items of interest is the playwright's treatment of this plot and what theme he would draw from it. The same plot has been and will be used many times; it is the treatment that makes it different and supplies its originality or artistic worth. Shakespeare is said to have borrowed all but one of his stories from previous authors, but he presented them so much better than had any of the others that he has never been seriously criticized for having done so. The treatment of a theme is equally as varied. It would be interesting to count—if one could—the number of television scripts that have proclaimed the theme "crime does not pay" in one way or another.

The same theme or story may be given a very serious or a very light touch. It may be an indictment of mankind or a tongue-in-cheek attack. It could point up a great lesson or show the same situation as a handicap to progress. The personality, background, and social or artistic temperament of the playwright is responsible for the treatment that he gives his story or theme. This we must both understand and evaluate.

If the dramatist is attempting to tell us something and that something is not clear, the play lacks communication and is open to criticism on that count. If life is complicated further rather than clarified, the play has fallen down as a work of art. This does not necessarily mean that we all get the same theme from a given play. Our own backgrounds or our ability to understand may be responsible for our differing with others on the play's full meaning. We may not like the way the playwright has presented his substance, or question its truth, or cite the dangers inherent in his work, but we should never leave the theatre without knowing what he was trying to say. It is the duty of the playwright, as an artist, to make clear to his audience what he thinks and feels and what he is trying to say or do.

It is, of course, not necessary that the story attempt to teach some great or accepted truth of life, but if it does, the play will have taken on a deeper and more permanent quality. That generally accepted truth is called its theme. Few of us would demand that every play teach a lesson. It is enough for some merely to furnish an escape or amuse the audience for an evening.

If an author chooses to write fluff and smart repartee, he should be given that privilege. If he chooses to write poetic drama, then we should accept the play on its own terms. We need not prefer it nor praise it nor go to see it, but we should not try to compare the work of the poetic playwright to that of the escapist or the discussion plays of those who use the theatre to teach or uplift. This was once expressed superbly by Bernard Shaw himself when he answered a critic who complained that a certain play was not great: "Its author never meant it to be a great play. The question is how does it rank with the type of play it is trying to be?"

To endure, a play should have a theme. It is sometimes suggested in the title as in *Loyalties, Justice* or *Strife, You Can't Take It With You,* or *The Doctor in Spite of Himself.* At other times it is found in a speech from the play itself, as in *Craig's Wife* when the aunt says to Mrs. Craig: "People who live to themselves are often left to themselves." Sometimes it is not so obvious but calls for closer study.

If the author whose desire has been to present a theme has done his job, we should be able to state the theme of his play in general terms and in a single sentence. The theme of *Hamlet* is the failure of a youth of poetic temperament to cope with circumstances that demand action. The theme of *Macbeth* is that too much ambition leads to destruction; of *Streetcar Named Desire* that he who strives hardest to find happiness oftentimes finds the least; of *Death of a Salesman,* the fallacy of building a life on shallow foundations; and of *Green Pastures,* that even God must change with the universe. Other themes that have been expressed in recent plays are: (1) It is impossible to give away all one's possessions, for even if one gives away the last final shred of his property, he still has the memories of the happiness he has brought to others. (2) One must come very close to death before he really knows how to appreciate life. (3)

Justice may be turned into a force producing evil as well as good, and that human beings, in their weakness, often exploit justice to satisfy selfish aims. (4) Evil ever rebounds on the doer, which may be only a more specific statement of the theme expressed in hundreds of scripts that "crime does not pay." (5) Man is just as good as those who know him believe him to be.

The statement of the play in specific terms is the plot or story that the play presents. Plot and theme should go hand in hand. If the theme is one of nobility or dignity, the plot itself must concern events and characters that measure up to that theme. As we analyze many plays, we find that some possess an excellent theme, but are supported by an inconsequential plot. A famous play of this nature was *Abie's Irish Rose* which held the stage for many years. The theme said: Religion is no hindrance to a happy marriage. The plot was so thin and both characters and situations so stereotyped that nothing measured up to the theme. This weakness was most obvious in the play's revival after twenty years.

Examples of the more frequent fault of superior plot and little or no theme come to us in much of the work of our current playwrights. They are known for their cleverness in making the most apt remark at the right moment. They are original and extremely witty in their conception, and their plays are very successful with a large following, but more often than not, they are utterly lacking in a theme or truth that will withstand more than momentary analysis. They are delightful, but ephemeral. An audience believes them only while being witnessed in the theatre. Consequently, these authors, although among our most popular, will not endure as artists, nor are their plays likely to be revived a hundred years hence. They but emphasize more strongly the axiom that a good plot or conflict is needed for transitory success, but a theme is more likely to assure a play of long life.

The greatest single criticism of our theatre today is that our playwrights speak but far too often have nothing to say. They lack purpose, skimming over the surface and not really getting at the reason for or motive behind the character's acts. This is, indeed, a weakness if the theatre is to meet its obligations as set forth in Chapter One.

Strategy and tactics

We have earlier discussed structure under form. The playwright's technique of implementing this portion of his form can be broken down into what is called *strategy* and *tactics*. Strategy is the over-all plan of the story as he conceives it. The carrying out of this strategy can be considered his tactics. It is his art of weaving in the exposition so that it seems a logical part of the story. He manages to give us all the details concerning the background and history of the characters and still makes it sound so natural and so much a part of the conversation that it is wholly logical and believable. This is also evident in his ability to create suspense or to bring in the element of surprise. Suspense is the most important single ingredient in any dramatic work and has been defined as that space of time which elapses between an action and the consequence of that act. Expectation is increased and emotion becomes more intense. The ability to hold us off the very maximum of time and not to strain us is a very important part of an artist's technique. Surprise has a value in dramatic worth equal almost to that of suspense, but surprise is not really dramatic unless it fits naturally and logically into the dramatic action of the play. Aside from being sudden and unexpected, it must be relevant to the action. Surprise for the sake of surprise is never truly dramatic. It must have a reason for its being. Further evidence of tactics is the manner of getting characters on and off the stage; of giving them sufficient time to accomplish the acts that are necessary to the dramatic action— to motivate their every action and make it logical, meaningful and in character.

Our great playwrights of the past have been masters in their strategy, in the laying out of an over-all plot. Some of them have fallen down on their tactics. On the other hand, our modern playwrights—especially those who have written for the motion pictures and television have shown great adroitness in their tactics but frequently have been less successful in their over-all strategy.

The observance of the playwright's success in this role is no small part of our evaluation of his technique.

Moral or immoral

There are undoubtedly those who would question the inclusion of this section under the play and the playwright. They might easily consider the whole discussion as a matter of taste rather than morality, or point out that one of the world's eternally unanswered questions is: "What is moral?" We realize fully that any individual's personal ideas of what is right or wrong—bigoted, narrow, broad or free as they may be—grow out of his own background, experiences, training, thinking and religious beliefs, and that these conceptions are influenced by time, by country, and by community; that they vary from family to family, and even within the family group itself.

This lack of any absolute standard only makes the playwright's task more complex. The community or educational theatre frequently finds its selection of plays greatly limited on this account. Even the professional field is often threatened with censorship. The motion picture and television are constantly faced with what they can do and say and what they dare not. It is most important that some artistically honest criteria be found for determining the morality of a play if we are to answer such criticism intelligently when it is presented by the more vocal segment of the audience whose personal moral code may not be compatible with what the playwright has written.

A long dissertation could be written on freedom for the artist or on a plea for broadmindedness on the part of the audience, but neither would help to answer the fundamental criticism that a given play or some part of it is immoral. What we must establish is some basic and honest measuring stick in the hope that the intelligent theatregoer can evaluate what he sees and hears and thus decide for himself. Few would deny our premise that the theatre is a reflection of life. It follows logically that its duty, then, is to picture life truthfully as well as artistically. It must not show only one phase of life or the little segment with which an individual approves, but *all* life of *all* classes and *all* groups and *all* personalities and *all* ages. We do not necessarily agree with the man who said: "Good plays are only written about bad people," but we do contend that if some evil does not appear in a play to conflict and contrast with the good, we do not have a very satisfactory play. It is *only* when the supposed evil succeeds or is praised as such that the play can justly be called immoral by any honest standard.

Today the items most often condemned by this small segment of the audience are the elements of swearing, drinking, and any suggestion of sex deviation or laxity. Why an audience, conscious of the fact that these "sins" do exist in the world and that one or more of them may even be practised by their own acquaintances or friends, should frown upon their appearance in the theatre is beyond comprehension. The fact that they do is common knowledge. Like the proverbial ostrich, those individuals would bury their heads in the sand or close their eyes to the things they do not want to see. They would judge the world by their own individual code of morality and on that basis would rate themselves as above reproach. By that same code, they would devaluate the moral standards of those who do not believe exactly as they.

These so-called "sins" need not be endorsed, but they should be recognized as existing in life, and if the artist is to portray life, he may need to include them. If the character is a swearing man or a drinking man, it is more moral and honest to picture him thus than to lie about his character. The audience need only remember that the playwright is writing about a particular character, not all men, and should see and understand that character as an individual. In short, it is the obligation of the audience *to judge the characters of a play in terms of life, rather than to judge life in terms of a particular play or character.*

Ibsen does not say that all women should leave their husbands, but that Nora—this one woman who is not permitted to be an adult, to have a personality or live a life of her own—does have the right to walk out of her home and leave her family.

Ibsen was writing in a day when the double standard of morals was the accepted way of life. He challenged that belief along with many other conventional ideas of his period. As Bernard Shaw pointed out, Ibsen was protesting "against the ordinary assumption that there are certain moral institutions which justify all means used to maintain them." He insisted that "the supreme end shall be the inspired, eternal, ever-growing one, not the external, un-changing artificial one; not the abstract law, but the living will." It is only natural that his plays disturbed both the typical audience-member and the typical dramatic critic of the nineties. Shaw con-cluded by saying what can be stated with as much truth today: "The plain working truth is that it is not only good for people to be shocked occasionally, but absolutely necessary to the progress of society that they should be shocked pretty often."

Only when a play directly or by implication makes an audience begin to question those laws of life which say: "Thou shalt" or "Thou shalt not" does the play become immoral. Just so long as the author has a true insight into the lives of his characters and pictures them as they are, the play is moral. If he makes his audience admire a vile character or invents excuses for situations that have no ex-cuse, lauds the villainy within the characters, allows weakness to be rewarded, or lies in any way about his characters, then we may say the play is immoral.

Chicago prohibited the playing of *Tobacco Road* with Henry Hull in the leading role on the ground that it was an immoral play. Any intelligent and honest person who saw Mr. Hull in this play must have felt that this prohibition on the grounds of immorality was unjust. Both Mr. Hull and the entire company made of that play a truthful, and for that reason a moral picture of life along Tobacco Road. After the language of the first few minutes had come to be associated with the characters as they were, one forgot the profanity as profanity. The play was conceived honestly, and the characters played with sincerity. It was far more moral for the author to employ the language he did than to have substituted something less fitting. It should be emphasized, however, that the discussion here concerns the production starring Henry Hull. Had the Chicago authorities forbidden the appearance of the same play as performed by some later companies, the ruling could have been more easily understood, for in their effort to capitalize on the publicity given the prohibition in Chicago and their appeal to a less discerning audience, these later companies reduced the play to uninhibited farce. They played it solely for laughs rather than the near tragedy intended. They made the most of all profanity and unsavory situations. All the aspects of the play that had been criticized were emphasized as such rather than as inherent in the characters of the unfortunate class of humanity portrayed by the playwright.

One may not personally like swearing. The motion pictures for many years steadfastly censored more than Clark Gable's hearty, "I don't give a damn!" as the tag line of *Gone With the Wind,* and thus played beautifully into the hands of those provincials who choose to believe that swearing does not exist. However, on the subject of drinking, equally as taboo to some in the audiences, the motion pictures have not only gone all the way, but have even carried it to the point of making it appear that by way of excess drinking one might even accomplish a goal otherwise unattainable. Television has followed the motion pictures very closely.

The whole question of morality is as involved as human nature itself, but the basis for determining morality in the theatre should be one of honest and objective analysis. Such an approach would demand that since a play purposes to give a picture of life, we must always measure the play *in terms of life* and never life in terms of the play. With this fundamental principle in mind we may then ask three specific questions:

1. Has the playwright lied about these characters? If at any point he has, the play, by our standard, is immoral.

2. Has the author permitted any evil or wrong to be rewarded? Have the wicked achieved their goal because of or through their wickedness? If so, the play may be left open to the charge of being an immoral play.

3. Has the author, in this play, clouded in the minds of his audience their basic beliefs in the idea of what is right and what is wrong? If he has, then again the play may be open to the charge of being immoral.

If we have been completely honest in judging the plays in terms of life rather than our own conception of what we believe life should be, and may still answer any of these three questions in the affirmative, then we have the right personally to consider this play as immoral. The mere presence of material with which we do not approve does not in itself constitute immorality by any just or artistic standard.

We would further emphasize that the artistic merits of a play are not necessarily affected by a decision as to its morality or immorality. The purpose of this discussion has been to find a terminology. We have merely presented what we considered basically honest criteria for evaluating the work of a playwright when his effort may not agree with the moral or religious beliefs of some of his audience.

Journalistic—literary—theatrical

There is one further question that should be given consideration in the playwright's technique. Is the play primarily journalistic, theatrical, or literary? Some may ask whether or not these factors might not be inherent in the substance itself. We, however, are proceeding from the point of view that material as such might possess any one of the qualities—or even all three at the same time. Once more, it is the treatment that the dramatist has given the subject that, in the final analysis, makes it fit any or all of the three terms—*journalistic—theatrical—literary.*

A play that can be justly called journalistic is one that is written for a given time and a given audience, largely because that particular type of play or that subject seems to be popular at that moment. The vast majority of the scripts seen on television follow a given pattern in any season—they cover crime, a particular kind of comedy, detective stories, westerns, mystery plays, historical pieces, foreign intrigue, or those fitted to some aspect of science-fiction. There is a demand and the playwright rushes to his typewriter and tries to satisfy that demand. They come from an exterior motive. They serve the same purpose as does our field of journalism. The audience is waiting for a particular program much as they await the daily newspaper. They choose the program or channel that fits their demand at the moment just as they choose the newspaper that reflects their own views on civic, religious, or political questions. The playwright writes because the public wants him to speak, and his work is as old and as dated tomorrow as the headline stories of yesterday's newspaper.

The purely theatrical piece usually chooses material of a little more longevity. It may last for several years, will bear seeing a number of times, and may even be revived as a period piece by another generation. It may not read as well as one would like, but it does play beautifully in the theatre. It has all the characteristics: suspense, characterization, excitement, and some truth or theme that gives it stability and meaning in the theatre. In fact, such a play is often called "good theatre."

The literary piece always has some inkling of eternity. It belongs not to a particular day or period, though it may use as its story an incident that has a date on it. The literary does not attempt to be novel or new or unusual. Its goal is not to shock its audience (although, as with Ibsen, it frequently does), but to reveal for them some truth that the author must share with them. Journalism seeks to be timely; the theatrical to be exciting. Both of these writers are interested in facts. The literary man is interested not in the facts as facts, but only insofar as they do represent recurrent truths of human existence. The literary playwright writes from an inward impulse. He has something to say, and he must say it. Tennessee Williams has summarized it very well when he says: "To snatch the eternal from the desperately fleeting is the great magical trick of human existence."

Playwrights have different goals. Occasionally a drama may possess two or even all of these characteristics, but the one that is envisioned in an "out of time—out of place" atmosphere belongs to the description of "literary" and has a greater possibility of living than one specifically dated by events or characters or one devised for the specific abilities of a given actor or a particular theatre's equipment.

It is important, in accordance with our premise of Goethe's three questions, that we may know something of what this author may have been trying to do.

TESTS OF A PLAY'S GREATNESS

We would not say that every play must be great. Frequently, the dramatist is not even attempting to write a great play. Few plays could meet the tests that one could logically set up for a really great play, for greatness may lie in many directions—as, for instance, in the journalistic, the theatrical, or the literary values we have just discussed. Nevertheless, we must try to find some formula that will help the beginner to determine whether or not the drama itself could stand alone or whether its success is dependent upon the work of the actors, the technicians, the director, or the over-all production.

We would begin by vigorously contending that every play must please its audience *now,* or it has failed *as theatre*—great as its other values may be. In the theatre, this *of-the-moment* response is of prime importance, for the theatre must capture and hold the immediate interest of its audience and give that audience the maximum of pleasure *at that instant.*

Harold Hobson has stated this very well in saying that "greatness comes to a play when (1) an intense experience in a fine mind is (2) translated with ecstasy into (3) effective theatrical terms." Mr. Hobson goes on to emphasize that by all odds the most important of these three elements is "theatrical effectiveness" and that without it there is no play, though it is the least literary of the three ingredients. He further points out that with all three we may have an *Othello*, with only the last two we have *The Importance of Being Earnest*, and with only the third we have a *Charley's Aunt.*

Frequently a drama that has great literary worth—or the first two of Mr. Hobson's elements—is revived on the basis of these values or because it has lived, as literature, for many years. In its day it may have also contained "theatrical effectiveness"; but owing to the nature of our times and the demands of our present audience, this most important element seems no longer to be present. Fortunately there is always a small audience of theatre enthusiasts who will find real enjoyment in a fine production of such a drama, but it may leave much to be desired so far as the majority of the audience is concerned. In our evaluation, such a production has fallen down as theatre, great as it may still be as literature. As critics, however, we should be able to recognize these different values and appraise them, rather than flatly to condemn the play as a play, or to deprecate the audience because of its lack of enthusiasm for a piece of literature that has withstood the tests of time.

Theatrical effectiveness itself has many degrees. Some plays may send an audience on its way, ecstatic with the most enthusiastic approval; others may have pleased in a quieter manner; some may have held the attention in performance and left food for thought in days to come. Still others may have held the attention for the moment but, in the light of the outside world, lost much of their lustre. These varying attitudes must be taken into consideration in evaluating any play's true worth.

In addition to Mr. Hobson's definition of greatness, we have a set of very valid tests given us by Albright, Halstead, and Mitchell in their *Principles of Theatre Art.**

* H. D. Albright, William F. Halstead, and Lee Mitchell, *Principles of Theatre Art* (Boston: Houghton Mifflin Co., 1955), pp. 74-76.

1. The intensity of the pleasure at the moment of perception.
2. The duration of that pleasure in retrospect.
3. The quality of the after-impression.
4. The quality of pleasure upon witnessing a second performance.
5. Comparison of the pleasure with that caused by similar compositions.

These tests are self-explanatory, and they can be very useful in our appraisal of a play's claim to greatness.

A third, excellent test is found in the five questions given us by Mr. Joseph Mersand.* For many years these have proved invaluable to the author of this book, who strongly recommends their application to any play when the question of its claim to greatness arises.

Does the play:
——possess universality of appeal in time and space?
——create living characters in convincing situations?
——stir, move, enrich, or transform us?
——express its thought in beautiful or appropriate language?
——teach life's meaning and strengthen our own hand in facing life's problems?

Regardless of what yardstick we may choose to use, we know that a play worthy of the term "greatness" must do more than merely hold our interest or entertain us for the moment. It must be really effective in some very definite respect, such as moving us emotionally with its beauty or with its truth, and it must have sufficient strength to sway our thoughts. To fall down on these points is to weaken its right to this distinction.

* Joseph Mersand, *The Play's the Thing* (New York: Modern Chapbooks, 1941-1948), pp. 32-39.

T H R E E

The acting and the actors

ACTING: DEFINITION—THE ACTOR'S SUBSTANCE—HIS TOOLS

Every viewer of stage, screen, or television is willing to pass judgment on the acting he has just witnessed, although the actor's art is less generally understood than any other art of the theatre. Standards are confused, principles are misconceived, and the technical problems are quite unfamiliar to the vast majority of any audience. The fault lies in that acting is too often judged according to personal whim rather than by well-defined artistic standards. It is frequently said that "the best acting is the least acting," which is to say that the best acting is so "right" that it seems not to be acting at all.

It is the purpose of this chapter to formulate some set of artistic principles that will serve us in understanding the actor's form and technique. First, we must determine what we believe acting to be, for there are many and varied definitions.

Acting has sometimes been dismissed by simply calling it "make-believe," and it is just that; for whether or not the actor really feels his role, he and we—the audience—are always aware that the experience is feigned and that there must be some conscious control of voice, body, mind, and emotion, that each actor must work with other actors and always remain a part of the scene, speaking lines that have been written down for him, memorized, and rehearsed. He must pretend to be something that he is not. But acting involves much more than make-believe.

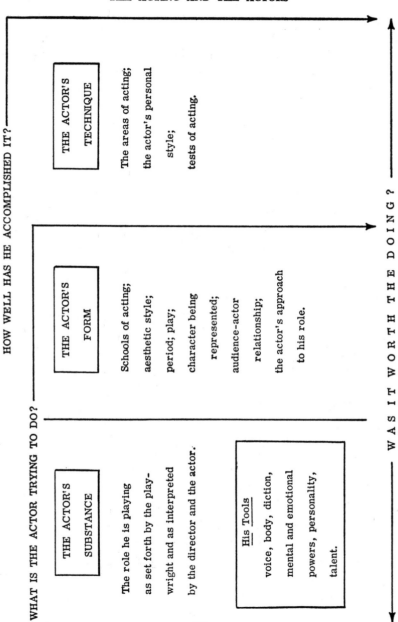

HOW WELL HAS HE ACCOMPLISHED IT?

WHAT IS THE ACTOR TRYING TO DO?

WAS IT WORTH THE DOING?

THE ACTOR'S TECHNIQUE

The areas of acting;

the actor's personal

style;

tests of acting.

THE ACTOR'S FORM

Schools of acting;

aesthetic style;

period; play;

character being

represented;

audience-actor

relationship;

the actor's approach

to his role.

THE ACTOR'S SUBSTANCE

The role he is playing

as set forth by the play-

wright and as interpreted

by the director and the actor.

His Tools

voice, body, diction,

mental and emotional

powers, personality,

talent.

Others prefer to define acting as "consciously doing on the stage the things that people do unconsciously in everyday life." Again, this is what the actor must *seem* to do; and if all plays were realistic in style, it might prove to be a very adequate answer to our question, but again it is not inclusive enough. What are we to do about the actor working in any aesthetic style other than the realistic? There are expressionistic, classic, and romantic plays, and these do not picture what we would consider as the reality all about us.

A third definition states that the actor "throws away his own personality—takes on that of another person—and makes that assumption appear real to the audience." This is certainly a satisfactory explanation of what some actors do. Who has not praised the work of an actor by saying: "He *was* Hamlet [or King Lear or Willy Loman]. I lost all thought of the man I know. His gestures, his voice, even his height were different." This is high praise, and the actor must have been convincing. But what of the many stars of screen, television, and stage who seem always to be themselves? What of the personality actor who draws millions to the box office? They, too, are actors. Where can we classify them and their art?

For our purpose, we prefer the definition: *Acting is the art of creating an illusion of naturalness and reality that is in keeping with the play, the period, and the character that is being represented.* Here we use the word "art," indicating that we recognize the actor's form and technique. We bring in the element of imagination and theatre in the "creation of an illusion"; we demand believability and truth with "naturalness and reality"; we qualify these attributes by permitting different styles and interpretations as we conclude with "in keeping with the play, the period, and the character being represented."

Acting—as an art—begins at that moment when an individual actor consciously sets out to have some specific effect on an audience. Acting is everything that he thinks, feels, and does, and the measure of his success is just how much and what kind of an effect he is able to create in that audience.

Micheál MacLiammoir in his *All for Hecuba* has drawn an excellent picture of what an actor is and must do:

> To be an actor demands a curious and complete surrender of the self and of many personal claims. More than any other art it is a rebellion against the mundanity of everyday existence. Far from being a copyist of life's surface tricks or a facile repeater of traditional antics, the actor should live with such delicacy, with such intensity, that he brings manner and style to all the unimportant trifles of gesture and speech, so that the eating of a fruit, the folding of a letter, the raising of the arm, the donning of a cap, all become, in his hands, images of significance, profound mirrors of character. To act is to live for a moment with an intenser life, to pass bodily into the sphere of sorrows and of joys greater than our own, to thrust the shoddy surface of what we call real life upwards to a transforming radiance; and while the painter must see and the poet and musician hear with passion before they hurry to canvas or to paper and ink, the actor must note all down with calmness and precision and must then give to the single moment everything he possesses, soul and voice and body, the inner and the outer selves.*

The actor, as an artist, finds his substance in the role itself. His chief source of information is found in the speeches of the character he would portray and in what the other people of the play say about him. Frequently, the playwright has given him some indications in character descriptions. If it is an historical figure, there is this additional source. Equal to anything that can be found in the script, there is its interpretation by the director or the author, if he is available. After all this material has been accumulated, there must be an agreement between the actor and the director so far as the role is concerned, and this decision might vary with what we in the audience *think* the author intended. Nevertheless, this over-all interpretation of the role by the director and the actor is the substance.

At this point the actor, as an artist, becomes unique, for he *is* his own instrument. His tools are himself, his talent, and his ability. Unlike other creative artists, he must work through and with his

---

* Micheál MacLiammoir, *All for Hecuba* (London: Methuen & Co. Ltd., 1946).

own body, voice, emotions, appearance, and his own elusive personal quality. All these he uses as a painter uses his paints or a composer his notes. As an interpretative artist he uses his intelligence, his memory of emotion, his experiences, and his knowledge of himself and his fellow men—but always he is his own instrument. Both in his form and in his technique he may choose to alter some aspect of this instrument in using himself as the channel through which the playwright's character is recreated and projected to the audience. We, as an audience, do an actor great injustice when we do not realize and properly evaluate what he has brought to the role by nature—physically, mentally, emotionally, culturally—as well as what he has managed to do with his personality and all it implies.

In addition to a normal body, adequate vocal powers, and some mental acumen, any good actor must bring to the theatre a further quality if he is to be successful, an essential element which we call *talent*. The first ingredient of talent is *imagination*, and without it one might as well give up the theatre at once, for acting is always the ability to respond to imaginary stimuli. One must relive almost any situation, appreciate and understand the thinking and the emotions of another individual, and express and project this imagined existence to an audience. As adjuncts of this all-important quality, he must possess *sensitivity* and *sensibility*. The first is a consciousness of one's own feelings; the second, a consciousness of the emotions or feelings of those around him. The two flow very naturally into the fourth, which Helen Hayes has so aptly called *human warmth*. There are degrees of all three, but any reputable actor must have a considerable amount of each.

The next important item is *stamina*. By this is meant health, physical strength, courage, determination. The theatre demands all these in anyone brave enough to join its ranks. To imagination, sensitivity, sensibility, human warmth, and stamina, we would add the "actor's five senses": a sense of the *mimic,* a *stage* sense, an *audience* sense, a sense of *rhythm and tone,* and a sense of *proportion*.

One's imagination is useless unless he can express for others what

70

that imagination has created for him. The stage and audience senses are often inborn. They involve a feeling for, and an "at homeness" on, the stage, and an understanding of its particular demands: the ability to sense the pulse of the audience, an inner voice that tells just how long a pause can be held or the split second when the next word should come after a laugh. Coupled with these talents and their training is the sense of rhythm and tone—the ability to pick up the proper rhythm when the one established in rehearsal has been momentarily broken by an unexpected incident on stage or in the audience. It is an inherent or acquired feeling for the play and its spirit, which can be adjusted to the ever-differing reactions of an audience and any of the minute human alterations of the established rehearsal pattern. The actor must at every moment be in tune not only with the whole production, but also with *this* performance!

Finally, there is the actor's sense of proportion, his ability to put first things first—to understand values both in and out of the theatre —his realization of what he owes the theatre as an institution personally and artistically, for a good actor must bring his best to every performance.

If talent is inherited, then great actors are born; but good actors, reliable actors, and even successful actors are developed if they, as individuals, possess sufficient desire, ample drive, and an ability to work harder and sacrifice more than in any other profession. Already the reader may be questioning these terms: *great, good, reliable, successful.* In our opinion, the difference between a great actor who is successful and a good or reliable actor who is successful is in exact proportion to the presence or absence of his *talent* as exemplified in the attributes listed above.

Talent is a gift, a God-given something in which he who possesses it should take great pride but for which he deserves no credit. It is a mystic and often indefinable element, a priceless ingredient that by some peculiar twist of fate and nature comes with birth and is found in many forms and combinations. In the actor, it may be a physical characteristic, a mental agility, or an emotional response. It may be a strange combination of ary and all. It means that the individual exists in terms of the theatre; his personality is capable of going vividly over the footlights; he possesses some contagious quality of voice, some great beauty of presence—a fine theatre-mask, a skin that takes make-up, eyes that can be seen, cheekbones that will not crowd them, or perhaps a sense of timing, a quality, a gift that is peculiarly theatrical and attractive to an audience. It must be present if one is to become truly great and rise to the level of Duse, Bernhardt, Garrick, Barrymore, Gielgud, Lunt, Fontanne, Hayes, and such comparable artists.

But this great and fortunate gift is not enough in itself—even to the most talented. All great artists have also possessed the second element—ability. This means the stamina to withstand hard study, dull exercises, the willingness to develop voice and body, and a command of one's intellectual and emotional powers. Such training demands determination, drive, sacrifice, work, work, work, and more work. It demands the sacrifice of personal wishes and hopes and other ambitions. If the hopeful actor possesses this second ingredient and just a little talent, he may have some chance of becoming a good actor.

We would not dwell overlong in our discussion of what acting is, but one of the most common misconceptions is that acting is easy—that anyone can act—that acting is just being natural on the stage. Nothing is further from the truth, for acting worthy of the name is as demanding, as creative, as difficult, and as dependent upon real discipline as any other art of the theatre.

In a sense, we have already touched upon the actor's technique; but this was unavoidable since he, unlike the other artists, must use *himself* as the form through which he expresses his art. These elements are all part of himself or his talent which he brings to the role. In a very real sense, they are the tools of his profession.

As an audience, we have done any actor a grave injustice when we have not distinguished the individual player and what he has personally brought to the theatre from the role that has been written for him and which he is now recreating, at the same time distinguishing this role from the artist and what he is doing, as an artist, to make that role come to life. These distinctions should be clearer after we have further discussed the actor's form and technique.

THE ACTOR'S FORM

Now that we have established what the actor is trying to do (his substance) and the tools with which he will work (body, voice, talent, and ability) we turn to his form or method of presenting this role to the audience.

Here we are concerned with the school of acting which he chooses to follow, the aesthetic or period style in which he will play, his actor-audience relationship, and his approach to the role.

Schools of acting

One frequently gets involved in discussing whether the actor who is completely different from himself on the stage is a greater or lesser actor than the individual who plays a role close to his own age and personality. If we are to be consistent in our criticism, we must start with Goethe's first question and not be concerned with which of these two schools is the more difficult or the more artistic.

What we would consider the actor's school is determined by whether he elects to go to the role that the playwright has written and make himself over, physically and vocally, to fit that imagined character, or whether he will bring the role to himself and make it over to fit his own vocal and physical characteristics. This is not an overt decision, for it is determined by both the actor's own personal talent and the demands of the role. It is easier or more natural for some actors to go to the role and thus become what we call *"impersonators."* In the motion pictures, our most well-known adherent to this school is Alec Guinness. Those who saw his fourteen different roles in *Kind Hearts and Coronets* will know at once what we mean by impersonation. Some actors on stage and screen possess the peculiar talent of being able to step out of themselves, take on the

73

personality of another person, and make it appear completely believable to the audience, even fooling an audience about their real identity.

Those who bring the role to themselves are called *"interpreters and commenters."* The characters they play bear a close resemblance to themselves in age and appearance, and they interpret the part without wholly losing their own identity. In our realistic theatre with its trend toward type-casting on both stage and screen, this school is much in prominence today. We would emphasize, however, that these actors are commenters on, as well as interpreters of, the role they portray. This "comment" is of the utmost importance in good acting, and it involves the art of the actor subtly giving us his own feelings concerning the character he is playing and all that character is saying or doing. He, as an artist, not only discovers, interprets, and projects the thoughts and emotions so that they are wholly clear to the audience, but he enhances that interpretation with his own particular talents, understanding, experience, personality, and charm. The character he plays will have taken on new dimensions as it passed through his mind and body to the audience. His voice may retain its natural quality, and he may use the same gestures that we have seen him use in other roles, but there will always be something new and different in the performance that makes this specific character an individual.

Owing largely to great deference to the box office, there is a third school of acting (often confused with the interpreter and commenter) which gives us what we choose to call the *personality actor*. He is common to all dramatic areas but is more frequently seen in the motion pictures and television. These actors have been defined by John Mason Brown as "the suave or tough, the charming or the brusque, the handsome or the portly 'straight' actors whose only, but whose quite considerable, talent is to be their off-stage selves on stage." Unfortunately, they are frequently the most popular and busiest actors of our day, for as personalities they have attained enviable reputations. Their great box-office appeal is due to their appearance, sex appeal, a physical or vocal idiosyncrasy, or some special quality that has a strong mass appeal. They are what Mr. Brown further calls "the most delightful and serviceable contributors to our theatre of understatement."

In studying the actor's form, it is necessary that we determine which school he has chosen to follow. This may be difficult the first time we observe an actor at work, for we may think that what he brings to us of himself is actually a part of the character; but on that first occasion, it is not absolutely necessary to classify him. After John Kerr's third Broadway appearance, Eric Bentley wrote in his criticism: "When I praised Mr. Kerr in two earlier plays, I thought I was praising acting. I now wonder if I was really praising a certain sort of personality—perhaps only a certain sort of sex appeal emanating from a pouting, indolent, insolent sort of face and a helpless, dead voice. In the next role he undertakes, let Mr. Kerr prove me wrong."

His form is easier to determine when we know the actor, especially if he appears in non-commercial productions, in which roles are cast contrary to the age group demanded. Non-commercial productions demand greater imaginary puissance and a further need for separating the actor from the role and the role from the artist.

Aesthetic style

In our definition of acting we placed special stress on the phrase, "the period, the play, and the character being represented." These are inextricably part of the actor's form and are determined by the aesthetic style of the play itself. The actor working in a Greek play will follow the more formal style of acting; in Shakespeare, the romantic style; in a play from the Restoration or eighteenth or even nineteenth century, there will be varying degrees of what may be termed the *declamatory style;* and in a modern play, the more realistic style of acting.

Shakespeare's admonition is good advice in every age: "Suit the action to the word, the word to the action; with this special observance, that you o'erstep not the modesty of nature, for anything so overdone is from the purpose of playing, whose end, both at the

first and now, was and is, to hold as 'twere, the mirror up to nature."
The "nature," however, may vary from play to play and certainly
from period to period; and it is the duty of the actor to conduct
himself so that he plays in key with the play as well as the period
and the character that he is representing.

This unity of aesthetic acting style in a production is, as we shall
later see, the work of the director, but the actor's projection of that
style is his job. On this count a realistic play is, of course, easier, for
the actors can find the nature they would interpret all around them.
They are presenting a world that is familiar to the audience. In any
other acting style the performer must use his voice and his body in
a much different manner. The bigger voice and gestures coupled
with the formality of a classic role or the abandon in gesture and
tone of the romantic style will frequently bring the criticism of
"over-acting" from the untrained critic. In the declamatory style an
audience may come closer to accepting the bombast or broad playing and recognize it as part of the play.

Sometimes as a part of and sometimes in addition to the aesthetic
style there is a production style. This is often referred to as "playing
the play" and it involves a unity of intent and projection by all
members of the cast. The production style is determined by the
director who may desire to play the script "for real" with the utmost
seriousness, or with a "tongue-in-cheek" approach. He may wish all
his actors to play as actors who are merely telling a story or he may
want them to seem to actually represent the characters they are
portraying. This approach will be further discussed in the section
which follows. The production style may mean that a farce is played
as a comedy or a melodrama as a farce, that a fantasy may be
played as if it were actually occurring or a romantic play done
realistically. Production style is found at its best in London where
actors may work together for a long period of time. We are told that
it excelled in the older stock companies where the same actors
worked together for years.

This unity of style in a production is one of the most serious
weaknesses in all the acting in our American theatre. It is due to

the fact that so few of our actors work long together and under the same director. This working together can itself bring about a production style that is consistent.

Actor and audience relationship

One of the earliest and most fundamental decisions the actor and director must make for each production is whether the actor's performance will be audience-centered (presentational) or stage-centered (representational). Will it be non-illusionistic (no attempt to give the impression that these events are actually occurring) or illusionistic that these lines and these emotions are all very real, the characters mean what they say and do, the events are actually happening). Although the playwright's script may suggest the proper approach, it is the actor's decision and the spirit of his playing that makes it evident to the audience.

In the theatre of the Greeks, Shakespeare, Molière, the Restoration, of the eighteenth and nineteenth centuries, the form was essentially audience-centered. The large audience, outdoor performances and the aesthetic styles of all these periods made it practically mandatory. The play was presented straight *to* the audience, almost as if it were another character in the drama—a character without lines to speak. The audience, in effect, was taken into the confidence of the actors. Such information as it should have was given out directly by the chorus, or through a soliloquy, and later by an aside. This form is common today in musical comedy, the vaudeville act, or the television skit with two comedians engaged in a verbal feud, but centering the whole of it directly to the audience. We call it presentational theatre. The old melodrama with the villain walking down to the footlights and confiding his thoughts to the audience was an exaggeration of this form.

Presentational drama can be either illusionistic or non-illusionistic. Certainly the actors in the roles of Oedipus, Electra, Agamemnon, Hamlet, Macbeth, King Lear and even Tartuffe intended that the audience should believe what they saw and should receive the impression that this situation actually existed and that the emotions and incidents were all very real. They were, then, presentational and illusionistic. This same technique—presentational and illusionistic—is used by the monologist as exemplified by Cornelia Otis Skinner or the late Ruth Draper in their one-woman shows.

On the other hand, many comedies such as *The Rivals* and *She Stoops to Conquer* and much of the eighteenth- and nineteenth-century sentimental drama might easily have been meant to give the impression of only a group of actors—rather than characters—telling a story. Each actor takes on the vocal and physical characteristics of the character he portrays, but he, the actor, is always present. It is almost as if he is speaking in the third person. This treatment is called presentational and is non-illusionistic.

When the theatre moved indoors, the scenic background became more realistic, the lighting improved and with it the intimacy of the production, and there was greater emphasis on the effort to give the impression of reality. The style leaned more and more toward realism or naturalism, and thus the stage-centered production came into existence. The audience ceased to receive the direct attention of the actors. The actors spoke only to each other. It was directed *at* the audience instead of *to* it. Eventually, an imaginary fourth wall was erected and the audience was, figuratively, looking through that wall at the actors. The actor's goal was to make the audience believe he was the character he pretended to be and that the story was actually occurring.

A play, then, can be audience-centered and non-illusionistic or audience-centered and illusionistic, or stage-centered and illusionistic. It is difficult to imagine a performance that was stage-centered and non-illusionistic, though that might sometimes occur. Occasionally, there may appear to be several different combinations of theatre form in the same production. In this instance it is the predominant over-all effect that should determine the classification.

Some plays can be nearly ruined because the actors have not understood, mastered or settled on a consistent approach as far as actor-audience relationship is concerned. An ultra-realistic modern play that depends upon the audience's belief and empathic response could have its very point shattered if one of the actors should suddenly step out of the illusionistic and stage-centered form and make a speech directly to the audience.

Interpretation, spirit, intent, director's or actor's goals, the playwright's purpose—all these help in dictating exactly how the actor will consider his role in respect to his audience. For our purpose it is necessary only that we understand the meaning of these terms so that we can judge more accurately what the actor is trying to do insofar as his audience relationship is concerned.

The actor's approach to his role

From the very first appearance of an actor down through the intervening years, there has always been a debate as to whether or not an actor really experienced or felt the emotion he portrayed while he was in the role. Interesting as such a debate is, an answer one way or the other is really not pertinent to our discussion. We are interested only in whether or not the *audience* feels, for to move the audience emotionally is the ultimate goal of the actor. This the actor accomplishes by his technique, for without technique the actor has no language to speak.

Consequently we shall do no more than define the two most common approaches to the art or craft of acting as it is practiced today.

One approach we hear so much about is most often referred to as *The Method* and springs from the writings of the great Russian actor and director, Constantin Stanislavski who, early in this century, recorded his theory of acting. Various translations and applications have given rise to a great controversy over what he really practiced or meant. Basically he is believed to have endorsed the importance of actually feeling—at least, in having the emotion start within—and the importance of producing only those outward gestures and movements or readings that grow out of that emotion. In short, the actor worked from the inside out and was possessed by the emotion of the role. The fountain-head of this acting theory is The Actor's Studio in New York and its director, Mr. Lee Strasberg.

The opposition to this theory includes those who would approach the role from a more objective point of view. They see acting as an art, but also as a craft. They would make a start from the outside and work in. After examining the role and coming to know the individual, they decide on his walk, his feelings, thoughts, and then consciously *act* or *do* the things they feel he would do. They might be said to follow the old James-Langue theory in psychology which said that action preceded emotion—that we run and then become afraid; that we talk rapidly and loudly and then become angry, and so on.

In the modern theatre these actors are commonly called *technicians* who use the *Technical Approach*. They act consciously by doing a specific thing for a specific effect. They do not disavow a certain amount of feeling, but they are most interested in control—physical and emotional. They cry for discipline and a technique that assures a performance that is consistent in performance after performance.

Great acting can and does come from either approach, and there are prominent stars who are strong advocates and followers of each. Our conclusion would be that either is acceptable (with the truth lying somewhere in between) just so long as the result gives the audience a consistently moving and convincing performance. If an actor's approach to his job detracts from the performance in any way, if he seems not to be in control of his body, his voice and his emotions, or if his technique shows—the most common criticisms of the two approaches—then the actor has fallen down as an artist. He is not a master of himself or the means to his end, all of which are a part of his technique.

THE ACTOR'S TECHNIQUE

In our discussion of the actor's form we may seem to have already gone well into the subject of technique. This is inevitable—at least by implication—for technique must be used to enhance natural talent. The very expression of the actor's form is by his technique. Sincerity itself is frequently as much a matter of technical expression as it is of feeling. Style is a sense of finish, which is only a synonym of good technique, and the finest technique is sensed rather than seen.

Margaret Webster, the eminent actress and Shakespearean director, expressed it well when she said:

When an actor rises to the greatness of his vision with the full armory of his physical powers—that, if his voice be great enough, is genius; and only when his physical prowess outruns the fervor and truth of his vision may he be labeled "ham."

Ham acting is technique in excess of emotion. Keep the two in proportion all the way up, and you will finally arrive at a theatre which is as exciting as it is honest, as theatrical as it is true.

An old actor summed it up: "Ham acting occurs when the actor gets caught using his technique."

Areas of acting

Regardless of which school of acting the actor may follow or what aesthetic style the play demands, or his approach to the role— there are three specific areas that he must control and on which his final performance may be judged. They are a part of his technique, and we call them the Areas of Acting.

> The Technical or Physical
> The Mental or Intellectual
> The Emotional or Spiritual

The technical or physical is similar, in a way, to the scales one must master in music. It involves the way an actor gets about the stage—walks, sits, gestures, moves, handles himself and the properties. It includes his breathing, vocal training and projection. It is the ease and convincingness with which he can *do* all that the audience sees and hears. All these attributes are basic to the actor's work. They can be taught and must be mastered before an actor can be really effective, for he must first be master of himself with his body and voice fully controlled.

The second area concerns the actor's mental approach to the role. He must have analyzed the character from every angle—understood his thoughts, feelings, and actions, his relationship to the play and the other characters. Again, his approach is not of as much importance to us as are the results—whether or not he is able to project a well-rounded, honest and believable character that would actually do and say the things we as an audience see and hear.

We have many actors who are highly successful in mastering these two areas. In the commercial as well as the non-commercial theatre there are those who never go beyond and who are considered "good actors." They are often referred to as "technicians" and even sometimes rise to stardom but they rarely attain the status of "great actors."

The third and most vital area of acting is the emotional or the spiritual. Unfortunately, there are many actors who never reach this height, and it is extremely doubtful whether or not it can be taught.

No one has ever sensed this third area as an audience in the theatre without being conscious of it. The experience may have lasted but an instant, or it may have pervaded a scene or an entire play. It may have been evident in only one actor—as is sometimes true in the community or educational theatre—but it is a quality that lifts the actor to a higher plane of creation and gives the spectator a special excitement or pleasure far above the ordinary. It furnishes those wonderful experiences in the theatre that one carries in his memory for years. Instances of its presence are legion in the annals of theatre history and stories about the great actors of the past, but there is not time to recite them here. If one has known the experience, the point is clear—if not, further discussion would not necessarily be of help.

Once again we quote John Mason Brown who has described this third area most effectively:

Then there are the precious few, standing at the top of their profession, whose high gift it is to act themselves, to adapt their spirits to the spirits of the parts they are playing, to possess and then to be possessed, by the characters they project, and to give them the benefit of their beauty and their intelligence, their sympathy and their virtuosity, their poetry and their inner radiance, their imagination and their glamour.[*]

TESTS OF THE ACTOR'S ART

It is now important that we consider some specific items in the work of the individual actor. No two persons will necessarily look for the same things, and it is doubtful if many will be conscious of the points we shall discuss during the performance. To do so might very easily be distracting on the part of the audience or an indication of some poor acting on the part of the actor. It is often only in memory that we realize just what it was the actor did to make us criticize him favorably or adversely.

In analyzing the work of the individual actor or the over-all effect of an entire cast, there are certain questions which should be considered. The first deals with the actor's personal qualifications, i.e., what he brings to the role. The next four concern the performance itself. They can be most helpful in pin-pointing details that might otherwise evade us. The final question deals with the actor's cooperative ability and unselfishness. It has taken on greater importance since the theatre began to demand a unified production.

These six yardsticks for measuring the actor's work can be of assistance in the discussion of any dramatic event, whether it be stage, motion picture, or television. In the chapters dealing with the playwright, the technicians, and the director, such questions would come under "Was it worth the doing?" or "Tests of Greatness." Since the actor is his own instrument they are part of his technique.

Six questions we would ask of every actor are:

1. What does the actor bring to the role in voice, body, personality, or as an individual?

[*] John Mason Brown, *The Art of Playgoing* (New York: W. W. Norton & Company, Inc., 1936).

2. Is his acting fresh?
3. Is his acting restrained?
4. Is his acting easy?
5. Is his acting convincing?
6. Does the actor fit into the production as an integral part of the whole?

1. *What does the actor bring to the role in voice, body, personality, or as an individual?* It may be imagination, a dynamic outgoing personality, temperament, a quality or style that is peculiarly his own, a voice or body that distinguishes him, or an authority that makes him master of all he does or is supposed to be. On the other hand, many of these factors may be negative. Above all else, each actor—on the stage—must be a distinct personality. Off the stage, he may be as ordinary as any citizen, but on the stage he must bring something definite to the role, and we as an audience must recognize and appreciate just what that something is. It has been said—and nowhere is it more valid than in the actor—that personality is an aura which surrounds those individuals "who are capable of doing some single thing extremely well and with consummate grace."

Let us first consider his *authority*. Does the actor have a complete command over his body, voice, and emotions? Is he above the role, or is he so involved in it that he lacks adequate control? An actor should be two persons, the artist and the character. The artist should ever be in the ascendancy, guiding and controlling the character he is presenting with a firm hand. It is evident in the way the actor handles emergencies, such as a late entrance, a missed cue, an accident on the stage, or an unnecessary disturbance in the audience. It is always evident in the actor's command of what we have already called *stage* and *audience* sense.

How effective is the actor with the use of his *voice* and *body*? The voice must be pleasant in its pitch and its quality. The force must be adequate to be heard throughout the auditorium. There is never an excuse for inaudibility. He must always speak without strain. The actor's diction, which includes articulation, enunciation, and pronunciation, should be sharp and clear, but must never attract attention to itself. Unless it is a part of his characterization, it must show no evidence of dialect or any particular section of the country. Any false or artificial note will instantly stamp him as insincere. He should have sufficient command of his vocal powers to impart the nuances that give originality to line readings—for unusual shadings which reveal hidden or new connotations in a line indicate not only a brilliance of conception, but a voice highly trained in the art of expression.

The actor's body must be completely coordinated. His movements must be graceful and his gestures used only to augment the voice. What he does physically must be effortless and never attract attention to itself unless that is the specific demand of the play. Every movement and gesture on the stage must have a purpose and a meaning. The slightest twitch of a finger or an unnecessary shift of the weight can become a distracting element. There must be a purpose behind any gesture or physical movement.

Does he possess an *individual style* or *quality* that distinguishes him as an actor? Individual style does not mean the use of individual vocal or physical mannerisms as such. Rather it implies the use of the actor's own body and voice *adapted* to the character he portrays, but adapted with intelligence and imagination as well as originality. It is the lending of his own instruments of interpretation to the role so well expressed by Mr. Brown in this third classification of actors on pp. 82-83. It is more than the actor just being himself. It is what the actor consciously does with himself. No wise actor ever attempts to copy any part of the style which is associated with another. No personal style is of any value unless it belongs to the actor as an individual and to him alone. Imitation is the kiss of death to any real artist.

As with all art, acting demands planning, precision, discipline. The only place for experimentation is in the rehearsal period. What the audience sees must not be haphazard, off the cuff, or the result of momentary inspiration. It must be worked out in detail. Authority would indicate control of the whole dramatic situation, and that situation might vary in some small way from performance to performance, but the over-all and general pattern of a performance should be as it was planned and rehearsed during the rehearsal period.

In this respect the actor in a motion picture or a filmed or taped television performance has an advantage, for another take is always possible. An actor's error or inspiration can be altered or used as the director and editor may choose.

What special characteristics does this actor possess to make him excel? What does he do that is distinctive? Such a quality in an actor may be a warmth, a coldness, a dry sense of humor, a winsomeness or any other personal attribute that distinguishes him as an individual personality. It may be something we feel or hear or see. It may lie in the quality of his voice or in a great talent for walking or in a tremendous personal charm or physical attractiveness. Whatever talent the particular actor possesses, it is worthy of recognition, for it is part of him and his art.

The actor's authority, his command of voice and body, his personal style or quality, and the sum total of his personality are the attributes he brings to the role as an individual. As we have said before, he is his own instrument and must be so considered and evaluated.

2. *Is his acting fresh?* Regardless of what the printed program may say, the events on the stage or screen are supposed to be happening now! No matter what period in history is being presented by playwright and actors, we have the right to demand that it give us what William Gillette called "the illusion of the first time." It is most important in the actor's work that each speech, each look, each action carry with it the evidence of its never having been said or done before.

Mary Martin on her five hundredth performance in *South Pacific* was so fresh and so new that it seemed as if she were experiencing every emotion and speaking each line for the very first time. Another important member of the company read each comedy line with the full knowledge, and practically with an official announcement, that here is a big laugh . . . get ready! . . . it's coming! . . . here it is, and . . . bam! Then he settled back complacently until the reaction had subsided and awaited the next response which he knew so well would come. It was obvious to the least critical analysis that his inspiration was gone and that the task of performing the role had fallen into mere routine

This "illusion of the first time" should be noticed in how the actor comes into a room, locates an object, reacts to the lines spoken by other members of the company, and in the tone of his voice. It can be especially evident in the fleeting expression of the eyes and face that appears just before the actor speaks a line. It is seen in the position of hands and feet, and attitude of the body. Not only is it of vital importance to the art of the actor, but also to sustaining the "half-faith" of the audience. It is the great test of the actor's thoroughness, his honesty, and his sincerity. Each audience has the right to demand this freshness, this illusion of the first time.

Observe how an actor makes an entrance or an exit. How many times one has seen a character merely come on or leave the stage. It is so obvious that he has been standing outside the door waiting for his cue, or that since the author has not given him further lines, he might just as well leave. On the other hand, great moments can be remembered in the theatre when an actor has made his entrance or exit truly meaningful.

Note how the actor sustains his role. Does the character grow and change as the play progresses?

Many times an actor will give all he has during the first act. This can only mean a plateau or monotony during the remainder of the play. He may also drop out of character when he has no lines to speak. Nothing can destroy the spirit of a musical that has been running for some time more quickly than to catch the disinterested expression on the faces of the chorus or those in minor roles during the song or dance of a featured player.

Much as we have insisted upon technique and important as it is to the actor, there is nothing more dangerous than the acquisition of a little technique. A few successful productions sometimes give the non-professional a feeling of confidence and a conviction that he knows exactly what to do on the stage at all times. This dependence on technique is also found in the work of the greatest stars of our stage, particularly after they have played a role for a great length of time. It is not difficult to detect that moment when the actor, as artist, walks off the stage both emotionally and mentally and leaves only the physical part of his character on the stage. Eva Le Gallienne has said that the actor's greatest problem is to re-create the original freshness, sincerity, and emotion of his character in every performance, regardless of how many he has given or what his own personal feelings may be at that time.

Again, the freshness of a performance will suffer more on the stage than in the motion picture, for the director may take and re-take the scene until the actor has given just the performance he desires. This is also true of the television program that has been filmed or taped. Live television can suffer in this respect, though it is not faced with the problem of the long run as is the legitimate theatre.

3. *Is the actor restrained?* We have said that we go to the theatre to have our emotions touched, that whether the play is romantic or realistic, we want it to happen in us. The final test of the actor is—does he make *us* feel the part? The actor's greatest asset in the realization of this goal lies in the matter of his restraint. He must have power within him, but it must be amply controlled. His job is to stir the imagination of his audience. Tears spilling down the cheeks are usually less dramatic than an effort at control. The blubbering close-ups of the motion picture are highly inartistic and far less effective than more restraint would be. The great actor hints at more than he declares. The real strength or power of any line lies in its tone. Watch how the actor builds within a speech or within a series of speeches—or even by pantomime—to a climax or crisis. Remember that sincerity or a crisis need not always be big. Sincere feeling is not big feeling, but rather depth and honesty of feeling. The word *ham* is greatly misused in the theatre—most frequently by those who would use it to describe something in acting that they

did not like, but do not quite know the reason why. They frequently confuse broad and expressive acting with over-acting. The first we need—the second is bad. We might almost say that the "ham" expresses small feelings in a big way, while the poor actor expresses big feelings in a small way. Any actor can be insincere, but only an actor with a big voice can be "ham."

Great acting is more suggestion than actually doing. It has been said that a good actor never fully portrays the emotion he wants an audience to feel but that he builds up to a particular moment, and when that moment arrives, the audience takes over, and the actor's work is done. Brooks Atkinson once pointed out that the real difference between a great performance and great acting was subtleness. This valuable quality of restraint is evident in the speaking of lines, in the handling of the body, in the grasp and expression of an emotion, in the smoothness and integration of all these elements. It involves never over-acting or over-stating, but rather relying on suggestion plus imagination and the intelligence of an audience.

4. *Is the actor easy?* The audience must be totally unconscious of any effort on the part of the actor. All hard work, so far as the audience is concerned, must have been done before the opening night. In performance the actor must be the master of himself, vocally, physically, and emotionally. His technique is there, but it never shows through. Whatever he does *seems* so natural that it is accepted without question. The perfect performance is one that seems to the spectator so easy and so right that he is tempted to remark that he, without training, could do as well as the artist.

Observe the success of the actor in the "art of doing nothing." This is one of the most difficult phases of the actor's work. It means that he must be on stage and a part of the scene even when the author has given him nothing to say and little to do, although he is still in full view of the audience. It has been said that acting is not as much acting as reacting, and there is no better proof of this statement than these moments of doing nothing. It is then that the actor's integrity, sincerity, and imagination are challenged, calling for great personal control and restraint. To be successful when given a speech and stage center is not nearly so great an achievement as to be always an important and necessary part of the picture without detracting from it and with apparently nothing to do.

Note the actor's sense of timing, how he uses the element of time through his mastery of pausing, phrasing, and holding. It has often been remarked that the actor's chief secret is his timing—an important facet of restraint. The term *time value* is sometimes given to those moments when words are not spoken, but the emotion and mood of the scene flow on. Anyone who has seen much theatre will remember particularly poignant moments when the actor played upon the imagination of the audience through the use of a gesture, a movement of the head or some indication of his feelings, suggesting a similar personal experience to the spectator which would have been lost had the actor resorted to the limitation of words.

There is no single distinction more obvious between trained and untrained actors than in their sense of timing. The inexperienced actor rushes forward, fearful that the audience will think he has forgotten his next line, but the true artist makes the most of every time value, knowing that there is greater power in the suggestion of an emotion than in its actual delineation, that he can create more in the mind of the audience by the correct pause than by any words he could speak.

Timing is most important in comedies. Watch how easily the actor plants a laugh, builds it, waits for it to reach the exact peak of its climax, and stops it at just the right split-second with his next line so that the play can move on. Observe closely the actor's sense of rhythm in this respect. At its best, it resembles a tennis game in the give-and-take between the actor and the audience as he varies his timing with their response, never breaking the basic rhythm of the play.

This sense of timing is of no less importance in the serious play. The actor's command of the pause, his use of the time value, his feeling for the exact instant for speech or silence are his most precious tools for holding and moving the audience. The actor's training in this respect is one of his most priceless possessions. It develops with the years and is the very core of his technique. For an audience not to recognize and judge each actor's facility in this area is to miss much of his art.

5. *Is the actor convincing?* Every item that has thus far been mentioned on the subject of acting contributes in some way to this question. The ultimate goal of every actor is to make the audience *believe* him and everything he says and does. His actions must at all times be rightly and fully motivated. His role must be synchronized with the whole production. There must be no inconsistency in his playing or in what he wants us to believe.

Sometimes characters carry such conviction in their playing that audiences find it hard to accept them outside the part. Actors have been hissed on the street or refused service in public places while playing the role of a villain or obnoxious character. The fault here, of course, lies with the audience that had failed in its obligation to dissociate the actor from the part he was playing, but the actor can not be accused of not being convincing.

The make-up and the costuming make their contributions to the actor's world of make-believe. So often his inability to apply make-up properly or to wear his costume naturally and with ease prove stumbling blocks in his convincingness. Make-up takes much study and practice and varies with the lights and auditorium that are being used. There is also the problem, especially in the non-commercial theatre, of the young actor or actress playing the middle-aged or older roles. One should make up for the middle of the house, but should strive not to apply it too heavily for the front rows. It is better to err with too little than too much. The professional theatre, with its emphasis on type-casting, has simplified the make-up problem to a great extent, but make-up is still an exceedingly important factor in the actor's being believed by the audience. Make-up on the screen is an art in itself. The camera is most difficult to fool, and, though type-casting eliminates the necessity of make-up much of the time, there are occasions when it is an important part of the total impression.

Both professional and non-professional players are often guilty of allowing their costumes to overpower them. It is most important to wear the costumes of a period play with ease. The Shakespearean ruff and cape, the tunic of the Greek theatre, the ruffles and breeches of the Restoration, the bustles and hoop skirts of the nineteenth century can bring havoc to a production unless the actors have learned to wear them as well as they have memorized their roles.

In a production of a Civil War play presented by a summer theatre company in the East, the mood was completely destroyed when the young lady arose from the sofa and turned too quickly in her walk to the upstage door. The front of the hoop caught on the corner of the sofa, and the rear of the hoop caught her on the back of the neck. The warm weather had caused her to reduce her undergarments to a pair of red shorts, and the audience suddenly had thrust before its eyes something that looked like nothing so much as the Japanese flag.

A criticism often made of an actor is simply: "I did not believe him." To avoid this condemnation is a vital part of every artist's work, for belief is a prime requisite of dramatic enjoyment.

6. *Does the actor fit into the production as an integral part of the whole?* Note how he gives a scene that does not belong to him as well as how he takes the scene that does. It is not always to an actor's credit to say that he stole the show. Many times he may have been playing to the audience in a bid for popularity rather than to have been a part of the scene as the author had intended. Famous stars have been small enough to make a movement, cough, drop a handkerchief, or by some other means attract the attention of the audience when the best interest of the play demanded that it be on some other player.

Sometimes the star in a professional production is guilty of upstaging the other members of the cast. This is unforgivable. The same error may be committed by non-commercial players without any intent of stealing the scene, although frequently with a little technique and some knowledge of the stage, they, too, have been known to do it deliberately. Part of the critic's work is to study each actor and understand his importance in the scene and then ascertain any indication he may show of being either the selfish actor who would stand out from the group, or the cooperative one who realizes that he is but a part of the picture and is wholly conscious of just what contribution he should make.

A story is told—which we shall suppose is fiction rather than fact —concerning three equally prominent and popular actors who found themselves playing a scene together. Actor A, who was downstage right, suddenly realized that Actor B at the apex of the triangle was receiving most of the attention and edged upstage in order to share the limelight. Actor C immediately realized that his back was on the audience and managed to get upstage of both the other two actors. Actor B became frantic and once more returned to the apex of the triangle. The same procedure was repeated, and before the scene was ended, all three actors were lined up against the back wall, turning their heads as they spoke each to the other. Once more we would emphasize that the story perhaps is not true, but it could have been, and, unfortunately, there are actors who could be guilty of such an indiscretion.

The preceding six questions must always be asked if we as theatre-goers would observe the art of the actors. Without asking them and without observing how successfully each actor has met each one of them, we are denying him his technique, and we are robbing him of his profession.

By now the reader may have discovered for himself some honest standard for his decision on the actor's contribution. Although acting does grow out of nature and is based on biology and all the human attributes and characteristics, the average man is no better equipped to evaluate the actor's art than any other art without proper training. Without such background he takes for granted that the actor's ultimate goal is to produce life so realistically that one could mistake the acting for reality. Nothing could be further from the truth artistically. Such duplication in any art is only deception.

The actor's worth as an artist should be based on our understanding of what he says *in addition to the lines he speaks,* for merely giving them their literal meaning cannot be considered acting. He must, in addition, imply what *he and the character are thinking.* Then he has, as an artist, begun to interpret. If he also portrays how *he and the character feel* concerning these lines, he has arrived at what we may call the art of acting.

A final and superior description of good acting comes to us from John Dolman who says:

> Good acting is neither wholly realistic nor wholly unrealistic. It is sufficiently realistic to be intelligible and suggestive and to arouse the necessary empathy; it is sufficiently consistent to be convincing; and it is sufficiently unreal to preserve *aesthetic distance* and to leave something to the imagination.*

When we, as an audience, have come to appreciate the art of the actor we shall be able to distinguish between him, his art and his role. With this artistic intelligence we shall no longer belong to that group who insist that any character whose death occurred during the play's action should not appear in the curtain call!

The motion picture and television actor

Although the names of the actors are used as an attraction to bring an audience into the motion picture theatre, the careful critic will realize that the actors themselves often contribute less to the motion picture than it would appear on the surface. Unlike the stage, the major contribution is often made by the other artists and by other means than acting.

Whereas the theatre is the art of collective acting, the motion picture is the art of individual acting and moving images. Not often is there need for much group work. We are excepting, of course, the many mob or crowd scenes that are so familiar. When an individual or small group becomes important, the camera moves in, and we have the close-up. This eliminates all except those few involved in that particular sequence. This is not possible on the stage.

The motion picture actor is often incidental to the background,

* John Dolman, Jr., *The Art of Acting* (New York: Harper & Brothers, 1949).

while in the theatre he must always be superior to it. It is not unusual for the inanimate object to be equally, if not more effective, than the actor. A close-up of a crushed hat or flower, or a broken glass can express stark tragedy. The camera can pan down on the turning of a doorknob and produce near panic in the audience. The impossibility of this on the stage is obvious. Herein lies a very important facet of the motion picture art which we should recognize and appreciate when it is done well. Sergei Eisenstein, famous Russian director, has called it:

the process of arranging images and feelings in the mind of the spectator . . . A broken ladder, a woman weeping, and a grave. . . . these can tell a complete story and create an emotional response.

In the theatre an equal result could have been acquired only through much dialogue and acting. Unless we are aware of this great assistance given the actors by the imaginative work of the director and technicians in the development and the projection of emotion, we shall have lost one of the principal elements of the motion picture art. We must have emotion—but we must not confuse it with acting.

The motion picture actor must work without any audience reaction, but he has as many chances as he may need to "get it right." The stage actor, on the other hand, inspired by the audience's response, has but a single opportunity in each performance. This does assure the assembled motion picture audience that it will see only the finest performance of which the actor is capable. On the stage there is always the possibility of human error, e.g., failing memory, a misplaced property, accidents of any kind. These deviations bring with them a new set of circumstances to be faced by the actor and an increased interest and element of surprise or enjoyment on the part of the audience. The tests for freshness and ease are not as valid in the cinema, for the two-dimensional photographs we observe may have been made months or even years ago. They are crystallized and changeless. In making those photographs the artists had many opportunities to get the exact effect they wished. We see only that result. As Mr. Rouben Mamoulian has aptly said, the audience watches the "future become the past" in a stage production and the "past becoming the present" in a motion picture.

From the actor's viewpoint there are further factors of differentiation. The stage actor must sustain a role over a long period of time, but he does have the opportunity of building an emotion logically from its very beginning through its crisis. On the screen few scenes last more than two minutes and more often are a matter of seconds in length, and they are not taken in sequence. The motion picture actor need not sustain his character except for a very short time, but he must be able to catch any degree of emotion without the opportunity of developing it from the beginning. He must start each scene cold. On the other hand, the stage actor must project to the very back row, both vocally and physically. The microphones and cameras solve this problem in the pictures, but the mental concentration must be far more perfect. The very proximity of the camera means that a single extraneous thought passing through the actor's mind during a close-up may register through the eye or some minute facial expression. Such details would be unseen by even the front row in the theatre. On the screen the actor must project and enlarge his gestures and facial expressions on the long shots and show great restraint on the close-ups. On large motion picture screens an eyebrow may be many feet in length, and the least quiver can destroy a complete mood. The actor must constantly adjust his work to the camera. It would follow, then, that our tests for restraint and convincingness might be equally valuable in either medium.

Actors on both stage and screen have found it possible to be successful in the other medium, but the techniques of each require study and concentration, both by them and by those of us who sit in the audience.

In the realm of television the stage and screen actors have each found their backgrounds to be both an advantage and a disadvantage. The great use of the close-up has been advantageous to the screen actor who was accustomed to it. The stage actor, with his projection to the back row of the balcony, vocally and physically, has found a need for adjusting to these new circumstances. On the other hand, the stage actor trained to the arena style of production finds this experience most valuable in the area of television acting; the stage actor can memorize a role or sustain a character throughout a long scene—he possesses a greater consistency in his control of body, voice, and imagination in contrast with the motion picture actor who has always played very short sequences and had the opportunity of repeating scenes time after time until the exact effect was attained. The cinema actor has been accustomed to numerous mechanical devices such as countless lights, numerous microphones, properties and the ever-present camera. The stage actor must adjust to being the servant of all this mechanical equipment and to being fenced in by it.

Both are faced with a far smaller playing area, the necessity for following exact movement, turns and angles as well as a most limited rehearsal period. The months usually given a motion picture and the weeks for rehearsing a stage production have shrunk to a matter of hours for the television drama. Television actors are conscious of these and many other details even while they work to develop a characterization, remember the lines, the exact direction, the idea of the play and the relationship to all the actors, keep one eye on the director and remember that their audience is really the cameraman—even should there be a studio audience present. Yet they dare not permit the discerning eye of the camera to show any of the frustrations which these technical elements can bring about. Add to all this the constant pressure of the clock ticking away the seconds, the vagaries of the sponsors, advertising agencies, and public ratings, and we can see why television acting is perhaps the most demanding of all.

Knowing all these problems of the television actor is important as background, but we should not allow them to enter into our final evaluation of his work. They are merely occupational hazards.

In television, especially in live shows, actors are far more the victims of type casting than in either stage or cinema. Both the difficulty and time required to change make-up and the risk involved of its being detected by the camera have eliminated the opportunity of actors playing characters unlike themselves in age or general appearance.

And now we would consider some of the special talents required in this difficult field. Even more than on the stage, the voice on a microphone must have a pleasing quality, a wide range, good articulation and a diction that does not attract attention to itself—unless it is essential to a particular characterization. It should also possess a style of its own and show rich feeling and intelligence. Through the voice and, visually, through the actor's body we get the sense of a speech, the purpose or intention of the character. There is no room for generalities in the reading of a line on television; the *specific* must always be in evidence. The actor must be especially careful of his word groupings, his emphasis and pauses. Variety is a vital factor. It is as if he were speaking to us personally, for he is physically so close to us, and our attention is so concentrated on him and him alone.

Characterization is of central importance. Because of the extreme proximity, this can be at once easier or more difficult. A greater control of facial expression and eyes, in fact the whole body, is essential. The slightest movement can be made meaningful or merely distracting. The close-up eliminates the possibility of any momentary relaxing that might be possible on the stage. A character in the theatre exists, primarily, in the imagination of the actor. By that actor's selection of physical and vocal externals he transfers that character to the imagination of the audience. He must know exactly what lies behind each speech if it is to be properly motivated. In any realistic characterization the television actor has a greater opportunity and more details with which to work—but with that opportunity he also has more responsibilities and a need for greater control.

These motives are the source of all action and reaction in theatre presentation. As viewers we are always interested in the motives of the characters. On the stage our chief interest is on the speaker and his actions. In both the motion picture and on television we frequently see more of the reactions of characters being acted upon. One can detect in any television program the great emphasis the cameraman, director, and even playwright place on reactions by focussing the camera on the face and action of the person being spoken to. This is an aid to both playwright and actor, for it pushes the story forward by telling the audience two stories at once. We are able to look inside the character's mind and to hear his thoughts.

Thus far we have considered only the straight dramatic programs, those that might fall easily under one of the four accepted types— tragedy, melodrama, comedy, or farce. The last three, as in both the other mediums, are much in the majority, especially melodrama and farce. Farce, which in television is often referred to as "situation comedy" is one of the most popular types. Here we find the same star appearing week after week in a slightly different situation. More often than not the leading roles are all played by the same actors. Within the program each character may have a name, but rarely do we remember or use them. The series is known by the name of the star and exists solely on his or her personality as a showman. Here the word *performance* as Mr. Atkinson has distinguished it from *acting* comes into even better use, for the programs are to television what the comic strip is to the newspaper. Characterizations are based on such simple and single traits as being extremely shy, very bold, most stingy, in search of a husband (or wife), unusually quarrelsome, meaning well but always doing the wrong thing, or just being an "average family." A companion to this "situation comedy" is found on a long series of morning and afternoon programs. The only difference lies in their melodramatic and pseudo-serious situations.

In either case the script, week after week, is practically the same —the situations varying just a bit from the previous episode. We would not condemn these cartoons *per se*. They may serve some purpose but must be recognized for what they are. Individually we may or may not care for the personality that is being presented, for the character he portrays, or for his particular acting style, but as critics we must view them objectively.

In this discussion we have considered some of the added problems of television acting and its variations as compared to the stage and cinema. What has been said should not alter our final decision on the artist's effectiveness as an actor, for the six tests of the actor's work are just as valid for the motion picture or television actor as they are for the stage.

The background and the technicians

WHO ARE THE TECHNICIANS?—THEIR TOOLS—THEIR SUBSTANCE

In our present-day theatre we have come to take for granted the elaborate and detailed scenery, the appropriate costumes, and the lighting that not only affords excellent visibility, but contributes so much to the mood of the production. One does not often realize that these embellishments are all comparatively new, and that for hundreds of years the script and the actors were considered as the only real essentials in the theatre.

The scenic background can be traced to a hut that stood at the rear of the Greek playing area. This small building was used by the actors to make the necessary changes to impersonate another character. Its basic purpose was *concealment.* When this structure was enlarged and decorated, especially by the Romans, the second purpose of scenery came into existence: that of *decoration.* During the Middle Ages when the theatre existed primarily in the Catholic Church, the various stations of the church served as a stage, and the third element of *mood* came into the picture. With the coming of perspective in the art of painting a fourth purpose was born—that of *suggesting* the locale of the action. Only within the last one hundred to one hundred and fifty years, and in our own realistic theatre, has the effort to *portray* place been a factor.

Historically the scenic background has come to us in the above

HOW WELL HAVE THEY ACCOMPLISHED IT?

WHAT ARE THE TECHNICIANS TRYING TO DO?

WAS IT WORTH THE DOING?

THE TECHNICIANS' SUBSTANCE

Mood, story, idea, or theme of play; purpose of the play as conceived by playwright and as interpreted by director and portrayed by actors.

Their Tools

line, mass, color, mood, materials, paint, jewelry, cloth, accessories, leather, light, shade, sound, camera.

THE TECHNICIANS' FORM

The aesthetic style or period of the play; the way this style is being expressed; the point of view of the whole production.

THE TECHNICIANS' TECHNIQUE

How the artist has chosen to express the form by his own interpretation; the use of color, design, personal style in area; effects by all technicians through color; personal style in interpretation; distribution of light; camera angles, and so on.

102

order. There are those who feel that it is also the order of importance so far as its artistry is concerned.

Until the theatre moved inside in the Middle Ages the only lighting was furnished by the sun. Once indoors candles were used for illumination which was sometimes altered by the use of colored silks or wine bottles placed in front of the flame for a special effect. The first real control of quantity in illumination during a given scene came with the discovery of gas in the mid-nineteenth century. Any real artistry in stage lighting is as new as our modern electricity and our ability to control its quantity, color and distribution. The electrician is the youngest artist in the theatre. He and his lighting equipment have been the greatest single influence of the twentieth century on theatre production.

The third technician is the costume-designer, although efforts to costume actors in the proper period or dress of the character being portrayed has been evident for only about two hundred years.

A fourth technician is often considered, though his contributions have varied in prominence from the Greeks to the present day. He may be responsible for the musical background, and many times his work should be given special consideration and study. In our present discussion we have included the work of the composer when a special score has been provided, with the technician in charge of all sound in the production. So far as the live theatre is concerned these are the technicians: scene designer, lighting designer, costume designer, and musical composer and/or sound man. A musical comedy, opera or revue would add the choreographer, the artist in charge of the musical arrangement, the lyricist, and others.

In motion picture or television production we find all the technicians listed for live theatre, and in addition the very important contribution of the cameraman. He is the artist responsible for using most effectively those techniques that particularly distinguish the motion pictures and television from the stage. He must possess a knowledge of all the technical resources and special means involved in the "shooting" process of cinema or TV production.

The substance of all these technicians is the same, namely, the projection of the story, theme, mood, or idea that the playwright has conceived in the particular interpretation given to it by the director. Each works with his own tools whether they be line, mass, color, wood, paint, cloth, leather, jewelry, accessories, light, shade, sound, or the camera with all its possibilities.

With his individual tools each technician has certain obligations to perform if he is to give the maximum assistance to the playwright, the actors, and the director in projecting the substance of the production. His form involves the use of his tools or materials in portraying the aesthetic style or period in which he speaks, his means of projection, and even the budget with which he works. His technique is how he uses these tools through the form that has been established, and, at the same time, speaks as an individual artist. It is how he expresses himself through his personal style or design in the medium of his creation, be it scenery, lighting, costumes, sound, or camera work.

THE SCENE DESIGNER

Obligations—form—technique

Today we would say that the first requirement of all scenery is that it must be functional and a part of the production itself. The obligation of the scene designer is to furnish a setting that will fit the action of the play in that it tells the background, social position, and life of the people who live in it. It must have the proper doors, windows, stairs, and furnishings called for by the story or movements that take place on the stage. In plays of a period other than modern, fewer details are necessary. A Greek play may be done in front of a stone façade or a set of natural drapes or in an outdoor theatre. Steps, platforms, pillars and the imagination of the designer can bring forth an ideal setting with the keynote of simplicity. The same may be said for Shakespeare. The setting must portray the type, the style, the mood, and the very spirit of the play. On the rise of the curtain, through the use of color and light, the audience should have a clear indication of whether the mood is one of seriousness or of lightness. In other words, the setting must help the actors tell the story, for the scene designer and the director must have come to a clear understanding regarding the spirit and mood or purpose of the production. Above all, the scenery must never attract attention to itself. The only time an audience should be conscious of the scenery—as scenery—is, perhaps, when the curtain first rises. The moment the play begins the scenery should fade into the background so completely that it is forgotten by the audience.

One of the most serious arguments against a very realistic set in the live theatre is that it frequently does detract from the actor and the play; that it weakens illusion because it challenges the audience to compare the make-believe set with life itself; and that in so doing it destroys aesthetic distance. On the screen we have come to expect—yes, demand—realistic scenery. It is a surface-realism, to be sure, but the scenic artist, especially in the filmed story, is expected to bring in the *real* thing, so far as the setting is concerned.

The first element of the technicians' form is involved with the point of view of the whole production—whether the purpose of playwright and director is to give a completely illusionistic and "for real" production or whether it is a tongue-in-cheek, purely "acted" play; whether it has been conceived as a period piece to be played as it might have been done at the time it was written, or whether it has been brought up to date. The type of play, whether tragedy, melodrama, comedy, or farce, will have a great influence on the forms that are used by the technicians. All these factors can be summed up in the over-all aesthetic style that is to be used, whether it is to be classical, romantic, expressionistic, impressionistic, realistic, theatrical, or pure fantasy. (See pp. 47-50.) At any rate, these are the channels through which the scene designer will work.

Few stage settings would ever fit solely into any single classification, for aesthetic freedom always permits borrowing from any source that will contribute to the total effectiveness of the artist's goal. The scene designer confers with the director and then proceeds to create the scenery that will best fit the needs of the play. Rarely does he think in terms of any particular scenic style. He does what he feels should be done, and after the set is completed, it is the audience who labels it. It is this labeling that presents one of our greatest problems in discussing scenery, and the difficulty lies in terminology. Unfortunately, few authorities are in full agreement as to the exact meaning of all the words they use to describe the settings in our modern theatre.

For our purpose we shall consider the six most commonly accepted scenic styles to be realism, simplified realism, impressionism, expressionism, theatricalism, and formalism. The first four lean in the direction of imitating life and, in theory, propose to help the actor develop and project the mood and spirit of the play. The last two tend to suggest rather than portray, serving only as a satisfactory background and, in theory, help the actor by staying out of his way. Our interpretation of each style will be presented in an effort to show how that style makes use of line, mass, and color.

Realism. The ultra-realistic set is an effort to portray place consistently, convincingly, and as completely as possible. There was a period when naturalism—which can only be defined as extreme realism—would have come first, but it is rarely seen today. In the realistic set great attention is given to small detail, and every effort is used to give evidence of reality. David Belasco even imported the authentic furniture of Madame du Barry with which he set the stage of the play about her life. At other times he insisted upon running water, a stove that actually prepared the food on stage, and such realism as knocking radiators. The sunsets which he contrived through lighting are still praised for their naturalistic beauty by those who saw them in the theatre half a century ago.

Such duplication of life and such lack of suggestion was and is sure to find criticism among those who accept the premise that all art is selection rather than representation, or that the theatre must *seem* real and not *be* real.

Simplified realism. This is an effort to use the advantages of realism, but to simplify them so that the setting may meet more accepted aesthetic standards. In the simplified setting no effort is made to fool the audience. If some detail is unconvincing, it is eliminated rather than to continue the search for a more convincing substitute. Some evidence of unreality may appear which is not a distraction, but an admission that the setting is only an illusion of reality. The goal of the artist is a suggestion of the exact locale rather than representation.

Impressionism. This gives only the impression of locale and carries simplification even further. It is what Jo Mielziner calls "implied scenery" and is more interested in mood than detail or any effort to do more than merely suggest place. It demands more imagination on the part of the audience. Because the element of exaggeration is almost inevitable, most impressionistic sets take on some form of stylization. An impressionistic set normally uses only partial walls and set pieces which are often silhouetted against a plain cyclorama. Doors, windows, and lesser details may be only indicated. This style of scenery is very effective in staging classical plays, or in fact almost any style of drama with the exception of the ultra-realistic.

Expressionism. This is the most difficult of all to describe, for it borrows from all the other arts by using music, rhythm, line, mass, color, and lights. The designer distorts the lines of the scenery to express mental or emotional distortion of one or more of the characters. Plastic forms, levels and sharp angles are used most frequently.

Whereas impression appeals principally to emotion, expression appeals more to the intellect. Very common a few years ago, it is used less frequently now except in combination with other styles.

Theatricalism. This is both the oldest and the newest style. Until the realistic theatre came into existence, it was the accepted practice in any theatre experience. This was especially true after the development of perspective in scene painting. It reached its height during the nineteenth century when wings and backdrops were frank admissions of unreality, even though they attempted to suggest the locale with their painted exteriors or interiors, including all minute details. A theatrical set today presents scenery as scenery. It may be decorated—attractive and in the mood—but it makes no pretense of being more than scenery. There is no attempt at any illusion of reality. It is only background and not environment. Actors act in front of it rather than in it, as they would in one of the above styles. The theatrical set is most frequently found in a musical comedy or revue.

Formalism. Formalism makes use of the natural background which belongs to the building, the theatre, or the auditorium where the play is being given. It employs neither representation nor suggestion. Perfect examples are simple draperies, the pulpit of a church, or an outdoor stage. Such a set is ideal for poetic tragedy. It was the only stage or setting used by the Greeks in their outdoor theatres or by Shakespeare in the Globe. Background is only background and not even expected to be considered as scenery. Formal backgrounds are very effective with the classics or in modern unrealistic plays suited to the presentational or audience-centered production.

In the following illustrations Don Swanagan, New York designer, has envisioned a realistic setting and then imagined how that same setting might appear if the generalizations concerning realism, simplified realism, impressionism, expressionism, and theatricalism were carried out. Formalism does not appear, because that style would use the natural locale and, therefore, no scenery, as we have here defined it.

Realism

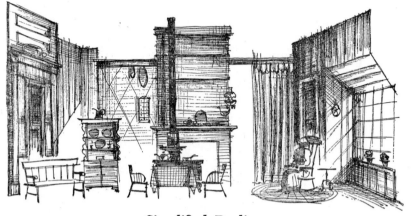

Simplified Realism

There are three contributing factors which may be used in conjunction with any one of the six scenic styles listed above. They are stylization, symbolism, and space-staging. In the confusion of terminology the most abused word of all is "stylization." In this book we should like to think of it primarily as an adjective which modifies one of the major styles.

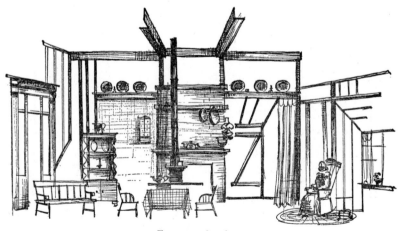

Impressionism

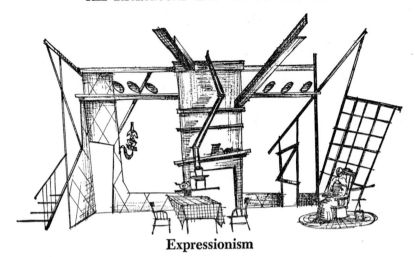

Expressionism

Stylization works with and depends on the imagination of the audience. It appeals to the emotion or to the intellect as the scene designer may desire. Its chief support is exaggeration of some kind with a special treatment of an established scenic style rather than being a style in itself. The very term *stylization* also implies illusion.

The scene designer may stylize according to the *period* of the play or the *mood* of the play. The first might involve designing a

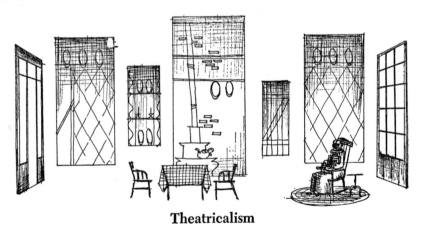

Theatricalism

near replica of the old Globe Theatre stage for the production of a Shakespearean play. In Shakespeare's day this would have been a formal setting, but now it would be *stylized formalism*. An equally imaginative designer might conceive a series of backdrops and wings to represent the various settings in *Ten Nights in a Barroom* as it was done in 1890. This could be *stylized theatricalism*. In his approach to mood another artist could paint an imaginative blown-up water color forest scene, depicting the wildest sort of trees and flowers for *Androcles and the Lion* which would suggest the tongue-in-cheek fantasy expressed by Bernard Shaw. This has been termed *artistic child's play*, for such a design would give the artist's impression of the play's mood and could be called *stylized impressionism*. The word *stylized* should thus always be used as a modifier and in association with one of our modern scenic styles.

A further contribution often used as part of a setting is called *symbolism*. This involves the use of some object which through its association will establish the thought, locale or mood. The imagination of the audience will then fill in the remainder of the setting. Such symbols may be used as a judge's bench for a courtroom, a blackboard for a schoolroom, a figure of the Virgin Mary for a religious mood. Further objects of symbolism could be a flag, a church window, a jail door, and so forth. Concrete symbols may become *symbolic impressionism*. Abstract motifs of a similar nature may thus lead to a *symbolic expressionism*. *Our Town* could be said basically to have used a formalistic background, but when the church window was projected on the back wall, or the soda fountain was implied by the use of two chairs and a plank, or the ladders suggested stairways, the scene designer was using a *symbolic formalism*.

The third contributing factor is called *space staging*, and if the director possesses sufficient lighting equipment and a satisfactory cyclorama—preferably black velours—he can do some remarkably artistic and imaginative work. Space staging involves a dark stage with a spot light picking out of the void the characters and scene involved. The lighted area may indicate anywhere or everywhere.

111

Space staging is usually found most practical and effective when a drama calls for a great many short scenes or when it is necessary for the action to move from one locale to another very rapidly. As much or as little as the designer may wish in the way of properties and scenery may be used to indicate locale. When, through space staging, an effort is made to suggest an exact place, with the use of skeleton scenery and properties, the scenery is referred to as a *Simultaneous Setting,* and more often than not is impressionistic in style. Any number of locales may be found on the stage—a country store, the pulpit of a church, a bedroom, an office—all adequately equipped to give a definite impression of place. Each can be brought into focus merely by concentrating the light on that particular area. A second and somewhat simpler effect is known as *Multiple Setting.* The principle is the same except that there is no effort to suggest exact locale, and the stage may be practically bare of scenery or properties. It follows more nearly the staging in an Elizabethan theatre with its outer and inner stage, balconies, and so on. As then, the lines are depended upon to indicate locale if that information is necessary. With multiple staging little more than light and characterization are used. Space staging can be used effectively in many plays but is less suitable in those that attempt to give a realistic representation.

We would emphasize that the styles in scenic design are constantly changing and that audiences should no longer expect standard sets, but instead look for imagination and artistry on the part of the scene designer. Experimentation with its possibilities is exciting and audiences can encourage it. Much has already been done by the educational and community theatres in this direction, and the scenic contributions of the professional theatre have shown marked progress in the past decade.

With this explanation of modern scenic trends, the following chart may help to summarize and further clarify the goals and means of the scenic artist in our theatre today.

These six modern trends in scenic art, plus the three contributing factors and combinations of any or all are a very important part of the scene designer's form. His technique or personal style is the

PURPOSE or GOAL

Helps actor to
portray
mood—
spirit—
emotion
by assisting him.

Helps actor by
staying out
of his way.

MODERN SCENIC STYLES

Realism (Naturalism)
consistent—convincing—complete

Simplified Realism
no effort at completeness;
unconvincing details eliminated

Impressionism
less detail—only essentials
to suggest locale and emotion

Expressionism
still suggests, but by distortion;
tries to portray feeling
in physical set

Theatricalism
Background decorated and
used as background only

Formalism
Building or surroundings
as they are

CONTRIBUTING FACTORS

Stylization
Exaggeration to
suggest
period or mood

Symbolism
One object
represents another—
or a great deal more

Space Staging
A light picks a scene out of a void
and illuminates a portion of a multiple or simultaneous setting which
may suggest or represent a specific
or a generalized locale—anywhere
or everywhere.

113

way he has personally expressed the central idea or mood of the play through the aesthetic style in his use of mass, line, color, levels, stage decoration or décor. To appreciate the technique of any artist one must constantly ask *how* he has accomplished his result and how original or creative he has been in his work—how it differs from what might have been done.

The motion pictures are rarely concerned with the subject of scenery as we have been discussing it. Their surface realism demands the real thing. This is not to say that it does not involve selection and arrangement, for the most effective background may or may not have been created or chosen. The latter is often evident when the living quarters of the characters in a motion picture are not in keeping with their economic status or position in society. The background sometimes seems to attract attention to itself by its beauty or some unusual quality. Rarely do the motion pictures try to use any but the realistic setting—even when the substance would seem to suggest some other aesthetic style. Television, on the other hand, has been more creative in this sense. As a result we have been given examples of some of the styles we have discussed. The result has proved to be both imaginative and artistic.

THE LIGHTING DESIGNER

Obligations—form—technique

It is necessary that the lights and scenery work in complete harmony, for one is most dependent on the other in the total effect, and both are only there to help the actor tell the story.

The lighting designer knows that the stage must at all times be sufficiently lighted to make for visibility without strain, but, as in all art, this visibility implies selection. The upper corners and walls should not be as brightly lighted as are the areas where the action of the play takes place. Good lighting must select and emphasize that aspect of the production which needs pointing up at any given moment. A doorway, for instance, need not be lighted during an entire scene, but it must be sufficiently illuminated when an important character makes his entrance if the needs of the play demand it, though the audience must not be aware of this change in the illumination. Artistic lighting should accentuate the proper emotional and psychological qualities of the play. Through the use of quantity, distribution and color the electrician paints the stage with light—much as a painter does his canvas—and in so doing creates a mood of mystery, impending disaster, warmth, frigidity, time of day, season of the year, or almost anything else.

In supplying adequate visibility, proper selection of emphasis, and the creation of a mood or atmosphere, the designer may do it realistically, or he may do it theatrically. This is his form or style. Realistic lighting would represent nature, and must have a natural source such as a window with its sunlight, a lamp, or a fireplace. These areas must be in brighter light than other parts of the room, for the lighting must follow the laws of nature. Light as seen through a window must alter with the time of day or year, but that alteration must be imperceptible at the time it is made.

For those plays that are lighted theatrically it is not necessary to consider the light source. Needless to say, such plays are the joy of the artist-electrician, for his imagination is the limit just so long as the lighting does not overpower the production itself. The theatrical use of lights is possible in the production of almost any style other than the realistic.

It is equally as important that the electrician eliminate any distracting elements such as a spill of light on the proscenium, teaser or tormentor, or a light leak from backstage. A poorly illuminated room, supposedly just off-stage and into which characters are to pass, can quickly destroy the illusion. An audience can be greatly disturbed by a flickering lamp due to a loose connection or the reflection of some light in a mirror or picture. Extreme care must be given to the light outside windows or when the impression of distance or sky is required.

In our theatre the lighting designer is an artist, and each of his effects is the result of careful planning, knowledge of human emotions, the specific needs of the script, the flexibility and limitations of his instruments, and his own creative imagination.

The lighting designer in the motion pictures or television has essentially the same obligations, though his work is often confused with that of the cameraman, for they must work together in perfect harmony. Where the stage electrician, working with the director and scene designer lights the stage for his actors and the audience, the motion picture electrician lights for the director and cameraman who, in turn, translate the story for the audience. Here it is the camera that sees, for on the screen the camera is really the eyes of the audience.

THE COSTUME DESIGNER

Obligations—form—technique

In any dramatic production today we have come to demand that the costumes must fit the period, the season, the locality, time of day, occasion, and mood of the scene. They must have the correct line and color to do the most for the character projection and for the individual actor playing that role. Each costume should be stage-worthy in that the lines and design are sufficiently exaggerated to carry over to the audience, and the costume should be so designed that it can be worn with ease.

The costumer's form is again determined by the aesthetic style and especially the historical period of the play's action. Certain eras are known for specific characteristics so far as dress is concerned. These would include such details as the midline decoration of the Egyptians, the chin ruffs of the Elizabethans, the immaculate collars and cuffs of the Puritans, the hoop skirts of the Civil War, the bustles and leg-of-mutton sleeves of the late nineteenth century, and so on. The artistic costumer takes these constant elements as dictated by form and simplifies or exaggerates as his artistic nature and the demands of the play may prescribe. This is his technique or his contribution as an artist. He must realize the vast range of color meanings and their psychological effect on an audience. He must be conscious of various combinations as well as the effect of light on pigment. Color must be considered with an eye to harmony, unity and contrast. Conflicting dramatic forces may wear opposing colors. Whichever technique is used must, above all, be done subtly. The good costumer knows that the actor must stand out against the set but that no actor, unless for a special purpose, must wear a costume or accessory that clashes with the set. In life we may not consider the color of the hostess's draperies or walls in our choice of a tie or dress, but on the stage it must be taken into consideration.

The actor's personality must be given special thought, both as it is and as it is to be in the play, for clothes are as personal as any other aspect of a character. Not only must they be agreeable to the temperament of the wearer, but they must fit the part he is playing. The Chinese have pointed out an interesting classification which they call the Yin and Yang theory, applicable to both men and women. The Yin is the sweet, quiet, sensitive, introverted individual, and the Yang, the forceful, strident, confident, forward extrovert. The first may seem to lean in the direction of those qualities which we class as "feminine" and the latter in the direction of those we consider "masculine." This theory further suggests that the proper dress for each personality is to emphasize his own type, such as ruffles or softer hues for the Yin, and tailored or more positive colors with an emphasis on the dark for the Yang. At the same time, each should borrow from the other with a median as the goal, rather than to go completely in either of the two directions. To do the latter might have a comedy value, and in some instances be exactly what was needed to portray the extreme masculine man or woman, or the extreme feminine. The same femininity or masculinity could be lessened, given its proper status, or perhaps even eliminated by costumes proper in both color and design.

As an audience we must consider both the costumer's originality in creation and execution as well as his projection of the dramatic significance each costume possesses. This is no small part of his technique.

THE MUSIC COMPOSER AND/OR THE SOUND MAN

Obligations—form—technique

In our discussion of melodrama we pointed out that the very term implies "drama with music." Even before the coming of melodrama, however, the theatre frequently incorporated some form of music as part of a production. With the motion picture a full musical background came to be a most important aspect until today more than ninety per cent of our pictures carry with them a complete musical score. Television adopted the technique, and the theme song of many a TV series has become synonymous with the name of the program itself. The living stage has borrowed from the other mediums, and original musical scores have become an important part of many modern plays, especially those of a more serious nature. In any discussion of the technicians we must, then, give some careful attention to the artistry of whatever musical background may be present; we must consider both the composer and those who interpret or perform it.

Regardless of the dramatic medium, the music must never stand out in itself. It should be only a background used to help in developing the mood, build the crises, set the period or sometimes establish the basic rhythm of the over-all production. That it has been raised to an art in itself is proved by the fact that we may not notice the music as such during the performance but will praise it when heard as a separate recording. The use of a familiar tune may prove a distraction, either by its very recognition or because of its association with some personal experience. A further distraction occurs when in a very realistic sequence the music is not adequately motivated by the actors.

Music at its best serves not as a mere substitute for dialogue, but as an emotional asset to the long periods of pantomime. Many times this lack of dialogue is not even noticed. To realize the preponderance of music and scarcity of speech in a motion picture, one needs but to listen without watching for some length of time. The musical

118

score to be praised, however, must always supplement and never supplant the acting. The less it is observed, the finer the artistry of the composer. In addition to music the theatre has become more conscious of sound effects in recent years. Authenticity is the keynote and perfect reproduction has become a necessity.

Only those sounds with dramatic value are included in either the stage or motion picture, but in the latter the element of sound takes on a different dimension. As an example, we cite the condemned prisoner in the death cell. To him the ticking of a clock takes on a very distinct meaning which the sound man is able to give the audience just as the prisoner hears it. On the stage this dramatic value would be lost. One can readily see the tremendous empathic possibilities that lie within the province of an imaginative sound man.

His contribution is even more important in the proper adjustment of the equipment as it relates to the musical score, the dialogue, or the combination of the two. His sound equipment may be his form, but the effective use of that equipment and the authenticity of the sound itself is his technique.

THE CAMERAMAN

Obligations—form—technique

We have already called the motion picture the offspring resulting from the marriage of art and science. It is obvious that its very birth was dependent upon the camera and the science of photography. Never for a moment must we allow this one essential difference between stage and screen to escape us. In essence, the substance and form of stage, motion pictures, and television are not greatly different. It is in the area of technique that the mediums differ, for technique is the basis of cinema production.

The two elements of the stage are performance and audience. The screen presents a third factor—often more important than either—the *camera*. Motion pictures are possible without a story, without scenery or even without actors, but never without the camera. That eye guides the audience to see just what it would have them see and interprets that material for them. In this sense, it is both the creator and the spectator, for it not only determines what we may see, but how we may see it. In its development the contributions of light and sound and their coordination have lifted motion picture production to an art in itself. This medium has unquestionably produced aesthetic achievements which would have been impossible in any other form of expression.

Rouben Mamoulian, motion picture and stage director, once said:

Let us remember that this is an age of science—a sort of scientific renaissance as compared to the artistic renaissance of old. Ours is becoming more and more a man-made world. In the past, science followed the dreams of artists. Today, incredible as it seems, the situation is reversed, and the artist is following the actualities of scientific inventions. Motion pictures are truly a modern art, and present an unprecedented phenomenon in history because they were brought to life not by the artist, but by the scientist. The most naive picture begins where the most advanced science ends. It is the highest achievement of scientific genius that makes possible the photographs that move, the shadows that talk, the mere a b c's of the screen.

Those who do not acknowledge motion pictures as an art because of this scientific and mechanical element seem to forget that all art in the world is subject to mechanics. After all, what is a piano, paints, chisel and marble, but the mechanics of musician, painter, and sculptor? Yet, of course, it is not tools that made such men as Wagner, Goya and Rodin, but the artistic result they achieved through their tools. The mechanics of a motion picture are merely the tools through which an artistic creation is expressed.*

The *cameraman*, then, must receive our sincere consideration as a motion picture technician. He can build a dramatic sequence without the use of actors, solely through photographic images. It is possible for him to create an intimacy through the close-up with its naturalness in both vocal powers and facial expression. This is an advantage denied us on the stage where the element of projection to the back row is so important. Medium or long shots can

* Rouben Mamoulian, "Stage and Screen," *The Screen Writer,* March, 1947.

either add to or detract from the total effectiveness, and the camera-man's use of them is a part of his technique. Color and light and their shadings are all within his province. Their psychological effect can be tremendous. At times the whole art of the motion picture or television comes closer even to painting than to the stage. These distinctions we must recognize and appreciate or criticize adversely as the case may be.

There are occasions when we find ourselves praising the photography even more than any other part of the picture. This is wrong if we are to follow our principle that the theatre is a synthesis of the arts. We must learn to appreciate the photographer's techniques and his ability to use his camera. We should understand the *cut* which is an abrupt shift from one angle or distance to another, or the *fade* which acts as a curtain on a stage production to disconnect one scene from the next or denote the end of a sequence. We should appreciate his use of the *dissolve* to connect one scene with the following one and yet to show the passage of time, or be conscious of the emotional strength in the *montage,* that rapid sequence or series of pictures which can build to a specific crisis. We should appreciate the kinds of shots, the variety, the angles and their total effect on the dramatic significance of the film. We should recognize his art, but only as it contributes to the total effect of the picture.

Filmed or taped television shows, with their greater freedom, come closer to the cinema technically—the difference being only that they cannot be as effective with the panorama, the long shots, huge crowds, beautiful settings or the chase. It is true that some television pictures have tried to incorporate these techniques, but the small screen makes them very difficult. This liability is often apparent when we see a regular motion picture—prepared for that medium—being used for television.

Due to the time limitations of the program and the size of the screen, the TV cameraman's responsibility is even greater than in the motion picture. He is second only to the director, and in some programs there is a camera director as well as the floor director who is responsible for the staging and acting. The two must constantly work together. If, as critics, we fail to catch the full impact of the camera as playwright, actor, and technician, we have failed to comprehend much of the cameraman's art.

As a playwright the camera serves as narrator, capable of prowling about the set and among the characters looking at everything. The smallest gesture, action or property can become the most important facet of the entire story. The camera can act in a most *objective* manner—as a third person—whose purpose it is to show the audience just what it would have the viewer see, and yet never becoming a part of the action. It can interpret the story, choosing just which character will at any given moment contribute most to the central idea, and making that character appear just as important or just as unimportant in the total composition as the camera chooses to make him. The camera can, in some situations as in a ballet, take on the attributes of another participant and move about among the performers as an integral part of the scene. This is called *subjective* camera technique.

As a technician the cameraman must have a keen sense of composition, dramatic values, sensitivity for feelings and a knowledge of psychology as well as art. He must know that too much movement of the camera can have the effect of making the audience dizzy, whereas too little will lead to monotony. There is a very short time —variously listed as twenty to thirty seconds—when the viewer can look at a single picture without losing interest. The cameraman must know just how much of the subject should be included in the picture for the best pictorial and dramatic effect—full body, from knees, waist, chest, or just the face and head. He must make the choice of angle—from side, front, back, or from below or above the subject. Psychologically and photogenically, as well as dramatically, this angle can mean much to the artistic or dramatic value. A camera shot from below can increase the size and importance of a character, both physically and psychologically; from above it can diminish his importance in relation to the whole picture.

There is more to choosing an angle, however, than merely a desire to do so. Each angle must have a meaning. A shot taken from high above the heads of two lovers in an embrace or from below could only confuse the viewer, unless it was an effort to use the camera subjectively and give the impression that someone was observing the scene either through a transom or from a position of hiding. The cameraman must appreciate just which view of the face is most pleasing, for individuals are often more photogenic from one side than another. He must be especially careful of the extreme close-up, especially with a young woman who may be playing a role younger than she actually looks. Few persons can stand to fill the screen with just face and head. The slightest blemish in complexion, scar, mole, or perspiration can prove a serious distraction. Costumes can be very attractive from one angle and quite ordinary or uncomplimentary from another. He must be sure that all pictures are adequately framed on the three sides—especially giving characters head room—which means ample room between the top of the head and the top of the picture. To cut a picture at the hair line of an actor or the ankles of a ballet dancer is a serious error. The cameraman must also choose the movement the camera will make—whether it will move forward or backward, to the right or left, vertically or horizontally. All his work must be without effort. All camera changes must be smoothly done and in complete rhythm with the action and movement of the story. As with other artists we must never be conscious at the time of his technique or how he is accomplishing his goal.

There are other technicians in motion picture and television such as the make-up man, the art director, the editor, set decorator, special effects man, and so on—and on. The long list of credits which comes at the close of any program gives some indication of what a tremendously cooperative art each of these mediums is, and we would not belittle the work of any technician. Each must make his contribution to the sum total or unified effect. If his work is a part of, and never apart from, that single impression—then it is as it should be. If the scenery, the décor, the lighting, the costumes, the make-up, the sound, or the properties attract attention to themselves as such, then they are in error, for we repeat that we should never be conscious of a technician's work while the production is in progress. To notice the scenic design consciously—to be suddenly aware of the lighting—the costuming as such—the work of the photographer—or the sound—is a distraction from the purpose or goal of the play. The work of each must be so "right" that it fits into the general background and is accepted in the spirit, style, or meaning of the production. Only in retrospect do we really appreciate the greatest artistry of a technician. Not to be aware of it—at the time—is the finest compliment he can be paid.

The direction and the director

DIRECTION: DEFINITION—TOOLS OF THE DIRECTOR

During its long history the theatre has belonged variously to each
of its many artists. The playwright, actor, scenic artist, electrician,
costumer, and director—each has had "his hour upon the stage."
At present that preeminent position belongs to the director. It is he
who is responsible for the selection, the organization, and the design of the over-all production. He is the leader, the coordinator,
the guide, the unifier of all the diverse elements that make up the
production. Any play that passes through his imagination will have
about it something of him.

It was David Garrick in the mid-eighteenth century who first
began to think of the production as a whole. After him we hear little
of the subject until 1874 when the Duke of Saxe-Meiningen established in Germany the idea of the director's discipline over the
production. It was his company which influenced the great Stanislavsky in Russia who in turn inaugurated many of Meiningen's
ideas in the famous Moscow Art Theatre. There soon emerged in
Europe what was known as the *regisseur* which is translated to
mean the "artist-director."

It has been wisely said that the director in our theatre today
decides *what* should be done by the actors and the technicians, and
that *they* are responsible for *how* it is accomplished.

HOW WELL HAS HE ACCOMPLISHED IT?

WHAT IS THE DIRECTOR TRYING TO DO?

WAS IT WORTH THE DOING?

THE DIRECTOR'S SUBSTANCE

The drama, itself, as written;

the director's interpreta-

tion of that drama as it

becomes a play.

His Tools

the play, the actors,

the technicians, the

audience.

THE DIRECTOR'S FORM

The choice of play;

the casting;

the aesthetic style;

the audience-actor

relationship;

the relation of empathy

to aesthetic distance;

the unification and

strengthening of the

seven pillars of a

fine art.

THE DIRECTOR'S TECHNIQUE

How he has emphasized the
theme and style of the production;

his use of stage movements,
business, groupings, and pictures;

his emphasis on the whole
production;

his handling of rhythm, tempo,
and pace;

his balance of empathy and
aesthetic distance;

his fidelity to the play's purpose
and his materials;

the over-all smoothness of
the production.

126

Harold Clurman, one of our most capable and sincere directors, has said that the director might be called the author of the stage production. He goes on to say:

Though the director does not act, he is, or should be, responsible for the kind of acting we see on the stage; though he does not usually design the sets, he is, or should be, responsible for the kind of impression the sets make; and this applies to everything else on the stage.*

Normally the director is the first to receive the script for study and thought. During this period he must discover the *exact* characters of the piece; search out their motives and relationships to each other and to the story; understand just where the play begins, how it builds through a series of crises to a turning point and a climax; just where the breaks will come. He must discover the mood or atmosphere; in short, determine exactly what the "something" is that the playwright has sought.

Once the director has made this discovery and has a full command of the script's substance and form, he must think in terms of actors who will fit into the various roles; of voices and personalities that will blend or contrast properly; of camera movements and pictures; of setting, stage décor, properties, lighting, sound and many other details that will help to interpret and emphasize this "something" he believes the playwright is moving toward. Basically this "something" is his substance.

In one sense the director is comparable to the conductor of a symphony orchestra, for, although he plays no instrument himself, he does unify the work of many individual performers into an artistic whole. He regulates tempo, commands every variation in the emphasis, and creates an interpretation. He constantly must think of the total effect, for he is the author's representative. It is his responsibility to see that each artist not only suggests a reality that we can believe so far as the play, the character, and the period represented are concerned, but also that together they *translate, interpret and express this reality so that it conveys the playwright's*

* John Gassner, *Producing the Play* (New York: The Dryden Press, 1953).

127

attitude. It involves playing a scene as farce, as high comedy, as melodrama, or as tragedy. It means playing it up, throwing it away, putting it across. It determines the style, the interpretation and the very spirit that the director feels the author had in mind as he wrote the script. In short, it is the director's responsibility to see that the actors and all technicians not only play the characters they have been assigned and furnish the necessary background, but that they also play the play that has been written for them. The director endows the written script with the necessary dramatic action and dramatic sound required to project the intellectual and emotional meanings as he interprets them.

Through the *script,* the *actors,* and the *technicians* he speaks to the *audience,* for these four elements are literally the director's tools.

THE DIRECTOR'S OBLIGATIONS AND SUBSTANCE

Since our premise in artistic evaluation is based on the three principles of Goethe, a director should be measured by the same criteria as the other artists. What are his obligations or goals? What is he trying to do?

Before we can fully answer this question we must point out that the theatre in America today falls under two general classifications —the commercial and the non-commercial. We have chosen throughout this book to use these terms in preference to professional and amateur because of the unfortunately derogatory connotation which has come to be associated with that word *amateur.*

In the theatre the actual distinction between the latter two terms is many times a matter of attitude, and the amateur performance, with its high purpose and sincerity, often matches and sometimes excels the work of many professional groups. A majority of our summer theatres, a few of our road companies, and an occasional New York production would suffer greatly by any artistic standards when compared with the best work of these non-commercial organizations.

The commercial theatre includes both the motion pictures and television as well as those living theatres centered on Broadway and the touring organizations which emanate from there. During the summers there are approximately four to six hundred "straw-hat" theatres, many of which are commercial. During the remainder of the year there exist approximately fifteen regular stock companies in various areas. The majority of these groups are recognized and operate under the rules of Actors' Equity Association, the union of professional actors. There are in addition some non-equity companies whose personnel receive regular salaries with the company maintained solely through the box-office. They are, therefore, classified as commercial companies.

The non-commercial theatre falls roughly into two classifications: the community theatre and the educational theatre. The first includes such well established groups as the Pasadena Playhouse, the Cleveland Playhouse, and prominent theatres in Houston, Dallas, Indianapolis, Charleston (South Carolina), New Orleans, Rochester (New York), Tulsa, Erie (Pennsylvania), and many others too numerous to be listed here. In addition there are the thousands of church, fraternal, civic and other drama groups which exist as art theatres, community enterprises, service organizations, and so on. The second group, the educational theatre, comprises, as it implies, the high school, college, and university dramatic endeavors, all of which are related to and usually underwritten by the institutions of which they are a part.

Every good director, regardless of the organization he represents, realizes there is only one standard of excellence in theatre art. He will not try to excuse the less-than-successful production by rationalizations of any kind. He knows that the inexperienced participants in an educational or community theatre may not come as close to scaling the artistic heights as does a professional group, but the first goal of each and every dramatic production should be the same —*a complete artistic success!*

In addition to this major obligation every director should challenge both audience and participants in a manner that will broaden their dramatic horizons but not out-distance their understanding, for, as a director, it is his duty always to keep the theatre both popular and alive.

Every director has certain obligations to the playwright whose script he is interpreting as well as to the play itself. Each is deserving of as sincere, as artistic, and as faithful a production as is humanly possible.

These are obligations common to every director, regardless of the theatre concerned. In addition, the commercial, the community, and the educational theatres each has its own separate goals and each individual theatre its own local needs. Unless we have given some thought to all these demands we have not been wholly honest in our evaluation of the director's work.

On the commercial stage and in the motion pictures the director must attract to the box-office a sufficient audience to pay all production costs and running expenses with some margin of profit for those producers who have underwritten the production. In addition he hopes to win the approval of a large portion of playgoers and the commendation of those professional dramatic critics who will comment on the production.

Although many of us feel that the commercial theatre often falls short of its obligation as an art form, we should constantly remind ourselves that it is also a profession and a business and as such the economic element is inextricably interwoven with the artistic. Realizing this, we may be a little less prone to dismiss a production as mere "show business." Theatre workers must eat and theatre producers must live, and the commercial theatre and motion picture are obligated to give the audience what it will buy.

Television also is a business as well as an art, but here there is an additional factor, for it must sell something besides itself. Only by the grace of the advertiser do we have a program at all. For this reason we must accept the commercial as inevitable, even though it does break the continuity of the story, and forces extraneous materials on a program that reduce its total effectiveness. The average cost of a television drama is $40,000.00, and someone must pay the bill. Since we rarely consider the cost and upkeep of the set itself, our admission is measured by the minutes we give the sponsor. Certainly this is small enough payment for some of the fine dramatic productions available.

In contrast to this commercialization of an art, the community theatres are usually organized, not for the purpose of making money, but to satisfy the creative desires of their members, to answer the frequent question of what to do with leisure time, and to bring together those persons in a community or group having the same artistic interests. The community theatre, interested as it is in the artistic success of its productions and in balancing its budget, exists also as a creative and social organization for the benefit of its members and its audience.

Any director who serves such a theatre is responsible to his organization for fulfilling these additional goals. They are not only justified, but are a vital part of the organization itself. Every member of the audience has a right to demand as fine an example of theatre as this group can give, but in his criticism he must not forget that the community theatre does have further obligations of its own.

In both the community and the educational theatre the director must be ever cognizant of those obligations common to all directors: a complete artistic production, a challenge to both participants and audience, and a conscientious loyalty to the script and the playwright himself. These two theatres have an additional obligation in common—that of bringing the living theatre to an audience with no other opportunity for such an experience, for many times these groups furnish the only source of live theatre to their respective communities. The educational theatre, particularly, must serve as a teacher if it is to justify its existence as part of the institution it represents. As such it possesses a special obligation to the student body who will attend the performances. The educational theatre director must give that group an introduction to and eventually an appreciation of the best in dramatic literature as well as good theatre. In addition he has a further obligation to the individual student who wishes to work in any phase of the dramatic program. The *desire* must, of course, be accompanied by sufficient *talent* and *ability*, but those students who possess these three important qualifications must each be given an equal opportunity to participate on a strictly competitive basis. This can eliminate what is known as type-casting. To take its place there is a far superior method for both the training of actors and the future of the theatre, and that is a mid-point between type-casting and mis-casting. This will also put emphasis upon a greater number of participants rather than the use of the same actors over and over again. The same is true in all other areas of the theatre—carpentry, costuming, make-up, lighting, painting, designing, or writing. Truly, in the educational theatre lies the gigantic opportunity to teach cooperation, teamwork, loyalty, and responsibility. Nowhere is each better realized than in the well-rounded dramatic production. The educational theatre director holds in his hands the great opportunity of helping his students to develop physically, vocally, intellectually, emotionally, culturally, and socially.

The director also has an obligation as a representative of the educational system and to the theatre as an institution that the plays selected should represent not only the best in type, style, and structure, but that they should come from every period of dramatic literature. His program should represent a sort of living library. At the same time, he must not reach beyond the depth of the students involved or the audience that he will attract. They must be challenged, but failure to meet the challenge can not only harm the participants but disappoint and lose the audience as well. The choice of play is of vital importance in every way. It must attract the audience as well as appeal to it after it is there. It has always been necessary for the theatre to build or create its audience. Today, if the stage is to survive, this must be accomplished by the directors in community and educational theatres. A theatre program that is too heavy can prove disastrous. It must begin with more popular dramatic material, for even if the director does prefer the romantic or classic styles, he is playing to an audience so young that they know only the realistic tradition. If they are to be taught to love the legitimate theatre, their early experiences must be exciting ones. To start on a solid diet of the greatest literary masterpieces can but play to empty seats, create dissatisfaction on the part of cast and staff and lose a potential audience.

Nor is this learning process ever complete, for each September brings to the campus a new group, and the process must begin again. A director in an educational theatre should not be judged on the choice of a single play or a single season. The programs can be more fairly evaluated only by considering three or four consecutive seasons, or whatever comprises the student generation.

Finally, there is the ever important and not to be forgotten obligation to the theatre director himself. He must satisfy his own artistic as well as educational standards. It can be done only after he has first considered positively the other demands, although at times it may be necessary to compromise here and there in order to give the most to the greatest number. Only in meeting the first four obligations can he as a director in the educational theatre meet the fifth, that of satisfying himself.

The director in the non-commercial theatre, community or educational, has five distinct obligations beyond bringing the best in live theatre to his audience and presenting an artistic production faithful in its interpretation of the author's script. These obligations are:

1. To entertain and educate the audience and also to build an audience for the theatre of the future.

2. To develop the talents and further the creativity of those active participants involved in the production.

3. To further the aims or purpose of the particular organization he represents.

4. To contribute artistically to the theatre as an institution and an art.

5. To satisfy himself as a director, an artist and a teacher.

Directors in countless non-commercial theatres throughout America are meeting these obligations most successfully. These organizations are the living stage's greatest hope for the future. The creed of one university theatre summarizes so well what many educational and community theatres are trying to do that it is listed here in its entirety.

Our Theatre shall endeavor always:
. . . to develop its students as individuals—vocally, physically, emotionally and culturally—rather than for the commercial theatre;
. . . to train both audience and students to appreciate the living theatre;
. . . to present plays that picture all phases of life and dramatic literature;
. . . to approach perfection in its own realm without attempting to imitate Broadway;
. . . to entertain but to contribute something more than mere entertainment;
. . . to encourage creative work in every phase of the dramatic arts;
. . . to add stature to the theatre in general, and to the college theatre in particular; and
. . . to be always *educational, challenging,* and *artistic!*

We must not dwell over long on this subject, but if each non-commercial theatre and its director is to receive the same honest critical evaluation as we would ask for all artists, it is necessary that some of the particular problems and specific goals be understood by the critic.

The director's substance is the script itself, and his interpretation of that script as it is brought to life in the theatre. This involves what he wants it to say to the audience as well as what he feels the author meant that it should say. He may change the period—the style—even the type. There are many opinions as to just what the license of a director really is. Some would contend that the moment the printed script becomes a living thing it has entered a new medium and that the director is equally as creative as is the playwright who wrote it. There are others who feel that a script should not be altered but should be interpreted exactly as the author intended—or as near to that goal as it is possible to do. We would not enter into this controversy nor voice an opinion on it. We are

134

primarily interested at the moment in what the director has tried to do.

THE DIRECTOR'S FORM

One of the first items we can consider here is the very choice of play. Here the responsibility in the non-commercial field is greater than in the commercial theatre. In the latter a director is hired to direct a particular play and can be held responsible for its selection only in that he did accept the assignment. If the play is wholly unworthy, then he as well as its producer may be justly criticized.

In the community and educational theatre every organization in each city or community is a case in itself and calls for a different program of plays. The fact that a play was successful in New York does not mean that it is a great play, and by the same token, because a play fails in New York or has not played there, is no indication that it is a poor play. The great hit of 1925 may or may not be right for a given theatre in 1960. The type of theatre demanded by the audience in a metropolitan center or on a midwestern college campus or a Texas community theatre is not at all the same. Locale and time are both involved in choosing the play that will attract the audience and do the most for it and the theatre at any given time or place. Audiences are often not ready for a particular play. To misjudge the temperament, desire or understanding of the potential audience in any locality can only ask for empty seats or an unenthusiastic audience, and either is equally harmful to the theatre and to the producing group.

A director's casting is part of his form. Producers in the professional theatre do sometimes insist upon special friends for certain roles, and actors have been known to produce plays only so that they might play a coveted part, even though they were not equipped to do it well. Nevertheless, the province of casting is normally considered to be that of the director. He may choose to type-cast and thus make his production easier to direct and more believable to the audience. On the other hand, he may choose to develop someone in a role by permitting the use of make-up to alter that actor's appearance and personality.

There also enters the element of interpretation. The director must have decided on what the role demands. With thousands of actors —and good ones—begging for parts, it is not unusual to read that the production of a play has been postponed because the director was unable to cast it. As an illustration, let us suppose a playwright has pictured a specific character as shy, retiring, bashful, or reluctant to speak up and express himself. Such a character could be interpreted by the director in any one of several ways accompanied by all the shadings of a human personality. He could arouse a warm sympathy by his quaint, shy and lovable quality; or become a broad comedy character at whom the audience could laugh boisterously; or he could be a stupid individual whom the audience might prefer to boot right off the stage. Each could be a logical interpretation.

Harold Clurman put it another way when he said that the whole meaning of the play, *Golden Boy* by Clifford Odets, depended on whether the director saw the leading character, Joe Bonaparte, as a fighter who had a gift for music, or as a musician who had a gift for fighting. Either is a matter of interpretation, the director's idea of the role and how he sees it in relation to the play and the other characters.

We may further consider the director's success by observing any obvious miscastings, actors who do not give evidence of being what they would have us believe they are because of their physical, their emotional, or their mental stamina.

Allied with the choice of play and the casting there is a special problem faced by most directors in the non-commercial theatre. They are often limited in the number of capable actors, both in experience and in age. This can limit their choice of program. Shaw, Chekhov, Pirandello, Shakespeare, Sophocles, Molière, Corneille and even many of our present-day writers make some rather extravagant demands of the actor. It would be unwise to choose a play—great as it may be—for which an adequate cast could not be found. We would emphasize that good theatre—regardless of what period it represents—can be exciting, but it must be well done if it is to excite the audience. The television and motion picture fields have been so very careful in this respect, and they have the distinct advantage of both unlimited talent and apparently unlimited funds to pay for it. If the stage is to attract this new audience—now accustomed only to the motion picture and television—its productions must be equally as exciting. The director who constantly strives to uplift the stage in the face of such competition is to be commended, but as a wise theatre man once said: "We are all for elevating the stage, but those of us who love the legitimate theatre would not suggest doing it by depressing the audience."

Along with the choice of play and the choosing of the cast the director's form is found in his decision regarding its interpretation. This involves the aesthetic style and the basic audience-actor relationship, whether it will be presentational or representational, illusionistic or non-illusionistic, all of which have been discussed in previous chapters.

Throughout these pages we have held fast to some basic principles—that all art is designed to give aesthetic pleasure; that the audience goes to the theatre to be moved emotionally; and that art is the result of selection and planning. There are many degrees of aesthetic pleasure, and many types or shades of emotion. The exact nature of the aesthetic pleasure and the emotional response of an audience is dependent upon the stimulus produced by the director's planning and arrangement.

An important part of his form involves the psychological and emotional reactions the director wishes to get from his audience, just to what extent he wants the audience to feel a part of the play, and how much he wants them to view it as an artistic work with a sense of detachment. This involvement—"a feeling into" or "a feeling apart from"—is a basic element in the director's form.

With the coming of the realistic theatre these principles have taken on much greater importance, and in them one may sometimes find the reason for his appreciation or lack of it. The "feeling into" we call *empathy* which means that the spectator both muscularly and emotionally experiences that which he observes. It happens in him, although he does not suffer the full physical or emotional strain that is experienced by the characters on the stage. To him it is a vicarious emotion, though he may even to a small degree participate in the same physical action as the actor.

During a performance of a mystery-melodrama a dignified and austere middle-aged man had become so involved in the situation being enacted that he unconsciously moved forward and raised his arm at the same moment the mysterious hand on the stage came out of the sliding panel. In doing so, he touched the shoulder of the young lady who sat directly in front of him, and she, being equally empathically moved, screamed uncontrollably. The whole impact of the scene was destroyed, for the distraction of her voice suddenly reminded the audience that they were only spectators observing a play.

In contrast to empathy is the "feeling apart," the detachment which permits the observer's attention to be held and his emotions to be touched, although he is conscious all the while that he is only a spectator. Herbert S. Langfield * has called this principle *aesthetic distance*. Every theatre production has some planned proportion of these two qualities. We must emphasize that emotion is involved in both empathy and aesthetic distance. Our interest is there, perhaps in equal degrees, but in one we are physically involved as far as our actual muscular reaction is concerned. In the other we are conscious of the fact that we are observing more than experiencing what we see. We are subconsciously more or less evaluating it as a work of art.

The motion pictures have long since sensed the value of both empathy and aesthetic distance. Every means of playing upon them has been used. Their melodramas have shown as much of the sur-

* Herbert S. Langfield, *The Aesthetic Attitude* (New York: Harcourt, Brace & Co., 1920).

face realism and personal physical reactions of the actors as was possible through the use of the close-up. Dramatic scenes are brought so close to reality that little is left to the imagination. A glance to right or left during a particularly strong sequence will show the contorted faces of the audience, the twisted handkerchiefs and sometimes even overt bodily action. If one has been too similarly involved in the situation to make this observation, he need only recall the muscular tension felt when a given scene has dissolved or faded into one which suddenly changed the emotion. The motion picture has likewise found great use for detachment in its musical extravaganzas, huge spectacles, and historical panoramas where it can excel so brilliantly. An example of empathy in a less artistic instance is evident in the athletic contest. It has been felt at a football game when the spectator's team has the ball within inches of the goal and less than a minute left to play. The spectator's neighbors may almost be pushed from the bleachers in his effort to help the home team.

Empathy is not always as muscularly active as it has thus far been described. Women may empathize in the leading lady and men in the leading man. Likewise, each may subconsciously feel it in his or her attraction for the player of the opposite sex. For this reason, casting in itself becomes a vital issue, for beauty, grace, stature, voice, personality, contrasts in coloring—all take on their own importance in bringing about the proper empathic response to each player.

In contrast, there is the detrimental empathy born of distraction or monotony when one's emotion is suddenly broken as he is snapped out of the situation he has come to accept or believe. This may be caused by a flickering lamp, a forgotten line or missed cue, a false cry or laugh, an extraneous sound, unstable furniture, or a characterization that the audience is unable to believe. Sometimes detrimental empathy comes from the audience or auditorium through coughing, a contrary reaction to an emotion by some individual, an overheated room, or some exterior element such as the illustration of the mystery-melodrama cited above. Television, with the many home distractions that accompany it, suffers here more than either the stage or motion picture performance.

Normally, the melodrama will require a greater degree of empathy. Its loosely drawn characters permit the audience a greater leeway in self-identification and the very nature of the situations carries a greater emotional force. Of the four play types, the least empathy is found in a farce, for here the spectator rarely wishes to identify himself with the situation he observes. To be actually involved in such circumstances would be unpleasant, but observing them in someone else gives the audience a perspective, and this detachment, coupled with a feeling of superiority, brings about the unrestrained laughter which we associate with farce. The same may also be said for very high comedy.

Empathy is found in varying degrees in comedy and tragedy. Both of these types are built on character and when well written and performed are so completely individual or removed from our experience that there is less opportunity for self-identification.

A play, if it is to accomplish its purpose, must happen in the audience. The degree to which it does happen is of vast importance and calls for a careful study by each artist, as well as some analysis by the spectator if he is to maintain a critical attitude.

Aesthetic distance is not the exact opposite of empathy, for it, too, involves emotional participation, but participation of a different nature. There is less of the muscular and more of the mental appreciation, although the personal aesthetic pleasure or enjoyment may be equal in degree. In the theatre it is most evident when we suddenly applaud a splendid piece of acting or a particular line. It involves recognizing the work of an artist and still believing in and being a part of a play, all the while conscious that it *is* a play and make-believe.

Artists have always been aware of the importance of this detachment. A painter puts his picture in a frame; the sculptor places his statue on a pedestal; the architect chooses to have his work set off with space about it. The conventional theatre of today depends upon an elevated stage, a picture frame created by the proscenium arch, a curtain, a brightly lighted stage and a darkened auditorium. It has not always been thus. Aesthetic distance in the Greek and Shakespearean theatres was sustained by the language, the nobility of the characters, and the more formal presentation. During both the Elizabethan and the Restoration periods in England aesthetic distance was largely destroyed when spectators sat on the stage and oftentimes participated in the action of the play by answering back and injecting their personal remarks into the production itself. The same has been true in certain periods of other countries.

In the eighteenth and nineteenth centuries actors acted as actors, and audiences appraised them and their art as individuals. Aesthetic distance predominated in many of these performances, and audiences thought in terms of the individual actor's interpretation of a role rather than of the character he was portraying.

Today much of the criticism we hear of the arena stage comes from those who are distracted by the proximity of the actors or by the spectators who can be seen on the opposite side of the playing arena. In one sense this might be considered a loss of empathic response, but it also is destructive of aesthetic distance.

Some productions today in our conventional theatres make use of entrances down the aisles, and even seat some of the actors among the audience. There are those who want to "put the play in the lap of the audience," and undoubtedly some theatre experiences could be enhanced by so doing. *Hellzapoppin* with Olson and Johnson still holds some sort of record in this respect. Entertaining as this piece may have been to many people, no one has ever called it artistic. On the other hand, it is possible to use the entire auditorium as an acting area and still maintain aesthetic distance, if the actor can remain a part of the play and never embarrass individuals in the audience by involving them in its action. Max Reinhardt attained this most successfully in *The Miracle*.

The type, nature, mood or style of the play determines how much empathy and how much aesthetic distance is to be sought. That answer lies to some extent in the decision of each artist involved, but more especially with the director whose task it is to balance one against the other artistically. This balance is one of the most important aspects of a theatre production. It involves not only the selection and arrangement, but the all-important problem of being just real enough to look *like* life and unreal enough not to *be* life, real enough to make the audience share with the players the feelings, emotions and thoughts of the characters, and yet to possess sufficient detachment to weep without real sorrow; in short, to share the emotions without actually experiencing their unpleasant aspects or becoming too involved in the production. Therein lies much of the theatre's art. It is also one of the greatest variables so far as our three dramatic mediums are concerned.

As a final element in the director's form we would turn to what John Dolman has called the seven pillars of the fine arts. While each of the seven is to be found in each of the arts involved in a theatre production, it is the duty of the director to strengthen them where they are weak and to coordinate the elements in the over-all production so that the final result presents: unity—emphasis—rhythm—balance—proportion—harmony—and grace. In our explanations of these terms we would emphasize that though each does possess a special meaning of its own, there is an inevitable overlapping.

Unity, as the name implies, is a oneness, a singleness of purpose. It would be absurd to place eighteenth century costumes in front of a realistic setting. If a director proposes to do Shakespeare in modern dress, he must have sufficient imagination to convey it throughout the production. Plays have been seriously criticized because they lacked a unity in style. The third act of *Our Town* by Thornton Wilder was so abrupt a break in this respect that it has never won the whole-hearted approval of many authorities. The same is true of *Liliom* by Molnar.

Emphasis is a pointing up or stressing of important points, a singling out of that which is most vital. It may be accomplished by movement, line, mass, color, force, or any other means the artist may wish to employ. Unity and emphasis together afford the most effective means of eliminating both distraction and monotony, the two enemies of attention. In so doing it brings into focus what we call primary or involuntary attention—that which we give automatically and without any effort whatsoever. Its counterpart is secondary or voluntary attention to which we must force ourselves. The theatre must always command involuntary attention only.

Rhythm is the recurrence of the accented beat. We are all creatures of rhythm throughout our lives. It is constantly a part of us; it is in our breathing, the beating of the heart, the days of the week, the seasons of the year. In the theatre we are more conscious of rhythm when it ceases to exist than we are when it is there. A fluffed line, an awkward pause, a break in the flow of the play, too long a wait for an audience reaction makes one suddenly aware that something has gone wrong. It is this element of rhythm that makes comedy so much more difficult to play than a serious play, for the overt reaction of those out front becomes a part of the over-all rhythm and that may change—if ever so slightly—from performance to performance. Actors must constantly be making adjustments to audience reaction.

Balance and *Proportion* are so closely related that it is difficult to make a distinction. They both indicate an equalizing of forces one against the other. Although it is not wholly true, we do sometimes—at least in the theatre—think of balance as being more visual, and proportion as a quantitative relationship. Using this connotation, we might consider balance as it relates to the stage setting and furniture arrangement, the symmetry and use of line, mass and color in décor.

Proportion may then be considered the relation of theme to plot, music to story, the relation between the two contending forces in the play's conflict, and so forth. The old melodramas, for example, fall down in proportion because they "stacked the cards" against the villain and in favor of the hero or heroine.

Harmony is a term with which we are all familiar. In the theatre it is the happy and smooth coordination of all phases of production so that nothing interferes with the basic meaning and purpose of the play. It is the ultimate objective of the artistic dramatic production.

Grace implies the minimum of effort on the part of each artist. No real art ever shows effort. It is the ease and facility with which the artist executes his work and masks his technique.

It is highly possible that during this discussion of the director's form the reader may have felt we were reaching over into his technique. We would emphasize that we have been talking here only about his decisions, his plans, his goals and the effects he wished to attain. In this respect we have considered:

The choice of play.
The casting.
The aesthetic style.
The audience-actor relationship.
The relation of empathy to aesthetic distance.
The final integration of the seven pillars of the fine arts.

THE DIRECTOR'S TECHNIQUE

We have tried to show that the actual *design* of a dramatic production is the director's form. The effectiveness of that design in production—visually, vocally, emotionally—is the measure of the director's technique; in short, his means of implementing or accomplishing his goals.

How a director has managed to emphasize the theme or style of his production should be observed and appreciated. There are directors whose greatest ability lies in serious drama or tragedy, and others who find their strength in comedy or farce. While it is pretty generally agreed that few directors can make a poor play seem great, it has been proved over and over again that a good director can improve on a poor script. It is also possible that he may not have done as well by the script as it deserved. Many a fine play has been ruined in the hands of an incompetent director.

No two directors can possibly give the same over-all effect, even if they were assigned identical casts and staging. A director's particular style or treatment is always there, evident in shadings of meaning, a change in emphasis, interpretation, characterization, or movement.

Each director may place a slightly different emphasis on the theme as the author has expressed it. He may even point up one of his own which will make the play infinitely more timely and appropriate. This was done most effectively by Orson Welles in his New York production of *Julius Caesar* during the peak of Mussolini's power. By emphasizing the dangers inherent in dictatorships and staging the play in a modern style with the conspirators in black shirts, the whole production took on an exciting, timely, new meaning.

In such instances the play may resemble the work of its director rather than that of its author. Max Reinhardt's *Midsummer Night's Dream* was more Reinhardt than Shakespeare. Any production by David Belasco was obviously a Belasco product. Margaret Webster is always completely honest in her interpretations of Shakespeare, but they do also carry the pictorial and colorful contributions that belong to Miss Webster.

Some directors like Welles prefer to do Shakespeare in modern dress. *Hamlet* has been seen with Ophelia drunk instead of insane, and Hamlet in a tuxedo smoking a cigarette. In *The Taming of the Shrew* Petruchio has arrived on donkey, on horseback, on a motorcycle, and in a battered old jalopy. Nineteenth century melodramas have been burlesqued or "kidded," as we say, and played perfectly straight as they were done in their respective periods. So recent a play as *The Constant Wife* could be stylized in mood with the actors playing the parts as actors with tongue-in-cheek and revelling in the wit of Somerset Maugham, or as a realistic comedy, the manner in which it was envisioned by Guthrie McClintic in the production starring Katharine Cornell. There are infinite styles in which a production might be conceived. This is the province of the director who is limited only by his own imagination.

We must always ask if every actor is playing in the same style or key. If not, the director is at fault. In a production of *Othello* the whole play lost its meaning because Othello used all the gusto of the romantic style accompanied by the rant of declamation, while Iago was played in a completely realistic manner. This error is more common in the non-commercial theatre due to the varied styles and techniques throughout the cast.

The word *action* in the theatre denotes only the dramatic action of the play which is inherent in the lines and story. Change of position on the stage is called *movement*. *Business* includes bodily gesture and the handling of properties. While both business and movement are executed by the actors and may have been created by them, the director is basically responsible for having permitted them to continue. Therefore, we may hold the actor responsible for the ease and truth of their execution, but whether or not they distract or are part of the play, scene, or character is dependent upon the director.

The director must always be responsible for furniture arrangement. This will, of course, do much in determining stage groupings and pictures which must always be the director's work. The famous director and teacher, Alexander Dean, often said to his actors: "You are the hands of the clock up there on the stage, but I am out here where I can tell the time." Stage groupings are of great importance. They must take into consideration the sight lines in the auditorium, so that every important phase can be seen by all the audience. They must show the different physical and psychological relationships as the play progresses. The stage must always have the proper balance, emphasis, variety, and dramatic meaning to help carry the story, as well as present an agreeable picture every moment. The stage is a continuously changing picture, but there must always be a focal point. Every movement and every bit of business must have a reason and a specific purpose.

The elements of under-acting or over-acting may be considered largely in the director's domain. Contrary to the commonly accepted belief, the non-commercial theatre is more likely to under-act and the professional to over-act. The director must have toned up or toned down as the demand required. It is in this area that many directors come in for their most severe criticism, for they think of themselves as creators in their own right rather than as interpreters of the author's script. A director may have a special flair for creating stage business, ingenious ideas of interpretation, or other embellishments through which he thrusts upon a play more of himself and his own abilities than are good for the production. Worthington Miner has said:

> If a director with a formula chooses a good play and attempts to apply the formula to it, he cheats the play and the author. The star director works for his star, the clever director and the director with a theory work for themselves, or sometimes . . . for something extraneous to the play. A conscientious director in normal circumstances works and can work only for the play.*

There is always the possibility that a company of players too long away from a director may allow much to creep into the play which was not a part of the original direction. Some two weeks after *Death of a Salesman* had been running on Broadway, it was completely re-directed by Elia Kazan because the mother, as Mr. Kazan stated, appeared to have lost her love for her sons. Mildred Dunnock, the actress playing that role, admitted that this was true, that she had become almost afraid of the boys because in their fervor they had actually been so rough in handling her on the stage as to hurt her physically. This subtle expression of her love for her sons may seem to the reader a minor quality, but it was so important to Mr. Kazan that long rehearsals and complete re-blocking of movement and business were necessary to restore this feeling of mother-son affection.

The director should be primarily interested in the play rather than the separate parts, in scenes rather than particular lines, in the over-all stage picture rather than in the individual actors. His job is to give the complete meaning and mood of the play and the changing relationships of each character to the play and to each other. Even though he may have to work with the individual, he thinks in

* John Gassner, *Producing the Play* (New York: The Dryden Press, 1953).

terms of the whole rather than any part. He strives for teamwork and unity in the over-all interpretation of the script. The audience is not conscious of individual bits or lines or characterizations. It feels and thinks in terms of scenes and meanings, crises, theme, and a unity of the whole. This is direction at its highest level.

If the author has not made all points perfectly clear, it is the director who must clarify and emphasize these details in his production. He may do it with movement, line, color, mass, force, or any other attribute he may choose. In short, he is a translator who uses all the arts of the theatre to correct any weakness inherent in the script. He has the final task of making everything clear.

There are three words which have oftentimes proved to be the greatest pitfall of the non-commercial theatre, the most difficult aspect of a play to explain, and perhaps the greatest single distinction between the experienced and inexperienced worker in the theatre. They are *rhythm, tempo,* and *pace.* Under *acting* we called this *timing.* These elements, when they are absolutely right, will cover a multitude of other sins and they are the director's responsibility.

Rhythm has already been defined as the recurrence of an accented beat. Its place in music is easily established and understood. It is quite different in the theatre because not only does it employ a broken rhythm, but the rhythm comes from many different sources. The emphasis of a word is, of course, an important part and more easily recognized, but the emphasis may also come from the entrance or exit of a character, the use of a light, an off-stage noise, a brightly colored costume, the gesture or movement of an actor, and many times—especially in comedy or farce—in an audience reaction.

The rhythm of a play is established very early and remains basically the same throughout the performance. The *tempo* alters, though the change may be ever so slight, with the entrance or exit of every character, many times within a scene, and constantly during the evening. The director who senses that a play seems to be running slowly and calls out: "Speed it up!" is utterly lacking in any knowledge of rhythm, tempo, and pace and their delicate balance. To speed a scene is merely to talk faster, to "railroad it" as it is called in the theatre, and all that happens is that the scene gets over more quickly. This, however, is the most frequent criticism of the untrained critic in the audience who proclaims: "The play was slow," "It seemed to drag," "The actors talked too fast," or "They didn't pick up their cues." All these are logical criticisms and may have been true, but the real fault is more basic. The chances are much more likely that the director had failed to point up a defined rhythm.

As with all good things, there is a danger in the other extreme. The director can become so involved in the rhythm of his performance that it stands out over the principal theme.

Pace is the relationship between the over-all basic rhythm and the ever-changing tempo. It is at its best when these elements are so perfectly integrated and all the speeches and movements of the actors so well coordinated with the audience reactions that the whole production gives the impression of complete smoothness. Strangely enough, the director finds his success in this respect easier with serious plays. This is largely because he can foresee the audience reaction to drama more easily than to comedy or farce. At least, their reaction is more constant. Comedy, and to an even greater extent farce, are most difficult to do successfully with an inexperienced cast. The comedy lines of the playwright receive such varied reactions from the audience that the actors must constantly cope with those changes and still maintain the basic rhythm that the performance demands.

They must alter their reading of lines or action within a single performance if they are to re-establish the rhythm as it was set by the director in rehearsals. If something unforeseen occurs on stage to alter that rhythm and pace, or the audience contributes a new beat through an unscheduled laugh or other reaction, or fails to supply the one that had been expected, it is only the actors who can once more get the play back on the right track. It is this combination of audience reaction and actors' recognition of it that can make a comedy so much more satisfying on the stage than in either the motion picture or television.

Rouben Mamoulian, famous motion picture and New York director, often establishes a rhythm through the use of a rocking chair, a metronome, or some similar device. He and others have been known to direct the play from out front with a baton. The pace of a performance and its integral parts are definitely in the province of the director, although his work is sometimes almost lost in the hands of an inept cast or the unexpected response of an audience. It is, nevertheless, part of the critic's task to ascertain what the director has tried to do with these intangibles of dramatic production.

Just what the director has done to establish the balance between empathy and aesthetic distance should be observed. This is an area where the audience may be even more likely to disagree among themselves on the quality of the director's work, for it involves so much the personalities, experiences, or memories of each individual concerned. This personal reaction toward the director's selection and balance may be equally true in tragedy or comedy. The final answer rests upon the director's own sensitivity, his knowledge of human nature and emotions, his own good taste, a strong sense of balance, and his stature as an artist.

It is no small part of the director's responsibility to understand the basic reason for the play's existence; that is, what the playwright was trying to say or do. Once he does understand this, he must then do all he can to emphasize these goals through his direction. There must be a fidelity to the central idea. All the artists must subordinate any personal desire to elaborate upon their work by including some personal talent or fetish. Even the playwright may have been guilty in this respect, and if this is true, it is the director's duty to handle the situation or scene so that it will not detract from the over-all meaning.

A most striking illustration comes from *The Cocktail Party* by T. S. Eliot. This play proved an enigma to many theatregoers in both England and America. The lack of clarity was partially due to a scene in the second act just after the psychiatrist had convinced a young lady that she should abandon the immoral life she was living and pay penance for her sins by joining the missionaries in some foreign country. After her exit, the psychiatrist, his wife, and secretary drink a toast to their accomplishment, but the lines do not indicate either the sincerity or the seriousness we have associated with the characters. It is this scene which has been one of the most difficult to rationalize with the remainder of the play. An unquestioned authority has reported that Mr. Eliot was repeatedly advised to delete this entire scene and that he even admitted it had no particular place in the drama, but added: "It is the sort of thing I do so well."

Every artist could make the same excuse for embellishing his work, but such embellishments would only serve to cloud or destroy the main issue. It is the director's responsibility to keep a strong hand on the reins, and since he has the final authority as to what will be seen and heard, he must possess a greater integrity and artistic sense than any of the others, for he, too, has "the sort of thing he does so well." Every artist should show a fidelity to his materials, and the director once more must make the decision. There are natural limitations to every art. Each artist must recognize and abide by them. He should not try to make a play look like a motion picture, an extravaganza, or a musical. He must not attempt to make the play designed as mere escape pretend to pass as a play of social significance. If he would present a solution to some personal problem, he should not make it appear greater than it actually is. If the play's chief emotion is only sentimentality, then that should be expressed as sincerely as possible.

The artist director will resist the temptation to borrow from the other arts and use beautiful costumes, settings, lighting, or music only because they *are* beautiful rather than because they help to emphasize his central idea. No artist needs a more consistent questioning of himself than does the director, and this questioning, if honestly answered, will always take him back to the meaning and purpose of the play and whether or not he projects them clearly and with the maximum but honest use of his materials.

Finally, the director is responsible for the smoothness of the whole production. This balance is one of his greatest contributions. Plays have been thrown completely out of focus when a leading actor was far superior to the remainder of the cast. The wise director, therefore, may not permit an actor to give his most brilliant portrayal of an emotion if the player opposite him is unable to rise to that height. The director must also balance the work of all the technicians. If the audience remembers setting, lights, or costumes at the expense of the play, the proportion has been faulty.

The director in our modern theatre is responsible for every phase of the production. It is he who determines the emphasis, mood, tempo, tone, the pointing up of some speeches or business, and the easing of others, the balancing of forces and characters, the elimination of distractions, simplification of lines or action that are not wholly clear, unifying the contributions of technicians, a complete new observance of rhythm, tempo, and pace, and, of course, the four tests—Is it fresh, restrained, easy, and convincing?

The alert theatregoer may come to recognize the hand of a given director, just as the connoisseur of art will know at a glance the work of a great painter, or the trained musician will recognize, after a few bars, the music of a well-known composer. These artists work alone, each striving for his own unity, emphasis, rhythm, balance, proportion, harmony and grace. The director, too, is working for all these qualities, but he must do it by harmonizing the work of many artists.

There is always the possibility that a cast too long away from the director may allow business and line readings to creep into the play which were not a part of the original direction. This frequently occurs with touring productions and especially with the non-commercial theatre where the actors do not possess the technique and discipline that will assure the same performance night after night. The motion picture is, of course, less likely to suffer from these errors than is the stage or live television, for in the former the director may re-take as many times as he desires, and we see only that which he has finally selected as most nearly representing what he wishes his audience to see.

For our present purpose, however, the recognition of the director's technique may be in what he has done so far as the following subjects are concerned:

How he has emphasized the theme or style of the production.

His use of stage movements, business, groupings, and pictures.

His emphasis on the whole production rather than individual parts.

His handling of the rhythm, tempo, and pace.

His balance of empathy and aesthetic distance.

His fidelity to the play's main purpose and to the materials with which he is working.

The over-all smoothness of the whole production.

The audience and dramatic criticism

AUDIENCE RESPONSIBILITIES

Throughout these pages the audience has always been foremost in our minds, for it is our firm conviction that the theatre exists for the audience and that every artist in the theatre works in the hope of sharing an experience with that audience by moving them emotionally and thereby bringing to them some measure of enjoyment or entertainment which is expressed through their sustained attention and immediate appreciation. It is this sought-for attention and appreciation that makes the audience an active participant in the sum total of any dramatic production, for their reaction, whatever it may be, is as much a part of the success or failure of any dramatic production as is the contribution of any other participant.

It is, indeed, the audience on whom we must depend for the very existence of the theatre, for artists themselves must be allowed, if not forgiven, some jealousy or at least reserve in their reaction to another artist's work. It is the exception rather than the rule for the elder artist to be without adverse criticism of what he sees or hears as the creation of the younger, and the younger is even more often critical of both his contemporaries and the older artists. This leaves the responsibility of cultivating, maintaining and protecting any art not with the artists themselves, but with their audience. For this reason a developed critical ability on the part of the audience is the very life-blood of any art—and most especially of the art of the theatre. To this end those who love the theatre must constantly endeavor to raise the standard of criticism above the level of mere impression or commentary. Criticism should involve constructive judgment and should be arrived at only with deliberation. Real criticism should be the conscience of the arts rather than a mere relating of personal impressions, which is only comment.

In the first chapter we listed the *obligations* of a theatregoer as entering the theatre with an ample supply of imaginary puissance, recognizing his own personal prejudices, giving every artist the right to work as he pleases, while trying always to distinguish between the individual work of the various artists, but first, last, and always, to apply the three questions of Goethe.

We also presented what can be considered as the requisites for an intelligent approach to dramatic criticism. These were: some knowledge of the theatre and dramatic history, a sense of theatre and its possibilities, some honest standard of theatre evaluation that includes both taste and discrimination, and an understanding of the form and techniques involved in the work of each theatre artist. In the chapters that have followed these requisites have been implemented by facts, principles, and opinions regarding the work of playwright, actors, technicians, and director.

We would now suggest that all this background be permitted to sink into the sub-strata of our being to be used only in general terms rather than specific, for nothing is so annoying as the bandying about of technical terms in general conversation or discussions. We would further suggest that the wise theatregoer open his mind when he opens his programs; try to see not only those dramatic events that promise to be good, but also those that are prospectively bad, for the poor productions sometimes may have more to teach than the great. (It is indisputable that bad art is helpful in recognizing the good.) He will, furthermore, see the plays he has sworn never to see; think again about the performance he approved so highly a few nights ago, and forget what the professional critics have said. In the theatre one should always be prepared for a surprise—many times it may be a very happy one!

LEVELS OF DRAMATIC CRITICISM

In a very real sense dramatic criticism can be said to exist on at least three levels which we shall define as the literary, the theatrical, and the practical.

The literary approach, sometimes called the Aristotelian, is interested primarily in the greatness or literary value inherent in the written drama, and critics have approached it in a variety of ways. Some have been most interested in its philosophical or sociological aspects. They would be principally concerned with its impact and contributions in respect to the individual's life and his relationship to the world, his problems and associations with his fellow men. Others have had more interest in the academic aspects of the script which concern the structure of the drama itself—the relationship of form and style or the techniques each artist has used to weld together the substance and form. Others give greater thought to the language of the drama, its characterizations or its theme.

A further analysis is made from the viewpoint of history. This would take into account the period in which the drama was written and first performed; the size and shape of the physical theatre; the evolution of the playing area and seating arrangement as well as the varying demands and moods of the audience during the centuries of the theatre's existence.

In any instance, this first level of dramatic criticism is primarily concerned with the written drama or the work of the playwright, and such an evaluation would be less interested in either its theatrical effectiveness or its popularity with the audience.

The second level is more interested in what the theatre can do for the drama when it becomes a play; how well it acts; what its psychological impact can be in the theatre. Its followers evaluate the script as a theatre-piece as well as a literary work. As aestheticians they are primarily interested in the magic that can be experienced in the theatre through its creativeness and the artistic use of imagination, lighting, scenery, and sound, for their interest lies in the beauty it can bring and the effect, aesthetically, it can have on mankind, theatrically.

The third level is concerned primarily with the practical theatre whose first interest is in making money through the attraction of great crowds. This approach is sometimes referred to as Shubertian or mere "show business." The name is derived from the famous New York producers who for many years made a business of the theatre. The critics who view a production on this level are interested purely in its popular appeal. They demand exciting entertainment which usually means escape. They insist on attracting great crowds. The theatre they endorse must cater to the masses and could sometimes be accused of sacrificing integrity and truth for popularity and appeal. It is the criticism we hear most frequently of the Broadway theatre as well as of the motion picture and television.

If Goethe's theory of art criticism is to be our premise, then our effort to formulate rules of dramatic criticism must recognize and evaluate all these various levels—the greatness in drama, the creation of aesthetic enjoyment through theatrical magic, and popular entertainment. It is our conviction that all are occasionally found in a single production; that sometimes none are present, and that more often than not there are variations of values even on the same level; that a vulgar piece often pretends to be better than it really is; and that tinsel, spectacle and applause can often mislead us.

PITFALLS IN ANALYZING DRAMATIC PRODUCTIONS

The theatre has always suffered, and perhaps always will, from the criticism of the inept and inexperienced. Every man, woman and child considers himself a just critic of what he has witnessed in a theatre. Though each may hesitate to discuss the worth of a musical composition, a painting, the lines of a cathedral, or any of the other arts, none will hesitate a moment to evaluate a dramatic production. He will speak glibly of the play and the acting and oftentimes the setting. This is perhaps the price the theatre must pay for speaking the language of the common man and for being the most democratic of the arts.

For our purpose we would choose the definition of dramatic criticism given us by George Jean Nathan as "*an attempt to formulate rules of conduct for that lovable, wayward, charming, willful vagabond that is the drama.*" It is just such rules or principles that we have tried to discover throughout this book. Let us hope that in using them the reader will not become the critic who feels he must always find a little bad in the best of things.

One of the most common dangers in criticism involves a desire to be clever, to say the smart thing or to play with words. The annals of critical writing are filled with devastating comments by sharp-witted critics who may have found the event less than satisfying.

A series of such comments is given here only for their entertainment value and certainly not for their instruction. Clever as these remarks may seem, and justified as they may have been, we would emphasize that they do *not* constitute dramatic criticism. Even though they come from the pens of some of our most noted critics, they may be classified under the pitfall of attempting to be clever. *The Reader's Digest Reader* lists them under the title, "When the Critics Crack the Quip."

When Mr. Wilbur calls his play *Halfway to Hell,* he under-estimates the distance.

. . . Brooks Atkinson

Katherine Hepburn [in *The Lake*] runs the gamut of emotions from A to B.

. . . Dorothy Parker

[Tank-town performance of *Uncle Tom's Cabin*] The dogs were poorly supported by the cast.

. . . Don Herold

[*King Lear*] He played the King as though someone led the ace.

. . . Eugene Field

If Booth Had Missed missed so completely that even the ushers failed to show up on the third night.

. . . George Jean Nathan

Perfectly Scandalous was one of those plays in which all of the actors, unfortunately, enunciated very clearly.

. . . Robert Benchley

Entire review of *Tonight or Never*: "Very well, then, I say never."

. . . George Jean Nathan

Excuse me for mentioning it, but a play called *Are You Decent?* opened last night.

. . . John Mason Brown

The second danger in dramatic criticism lies in the fact that the critic so often cites picayune details or minor accidents in performance rather than searching for the real dramatic values. If ever the old expression about not seeing the forest for the trees is applicable, it is here. The untrained critic will pounce on such small items as a fluffed line, a delayed light cue, a property not wholly authentic, some slight discrepancy in make-up, a ravelling on a costume, or some similar detail not worthy of mention. If such items in the total picture have been so numerous or so blatant as to denote carelessness on the part of the artists or to take precedence over plot, theme, acting, setting, or direction, that is another story. In this case, adverse criticism is justified, although the details themselves need not be mentioned individually.

First nights in any theatre are often chaotic affairs. The nervousness of the entire company and the importance of the event often produce many unforeseen accidents, but discerning critics never allow them to sway their opinion of the production as a whole.

This second danger may easily lead into a third which is typical especially of the novice, although there are seasoned playgoers and professional critics who seem never to really enjoy a dramatic event because they have become so involved in looking for something wrong that they miss the more valuable points of the art itself. They are the unfortunate souls who have the same trouble as the man in E. B. White's verse:

* © 1925, The New Yorker Magazine, Inc.

DEFINITIONS
Critic
The critic leaves at curtain fall
To find, in starting to review it,
He scarcely saw the play at all
For watching his reaction to it.
E.B.W.

The intelligent playgoer soon finds that this is only an early phase in his development. Soon he ceases to think of details and begins to study the production as a whole. Then criticism will take its logical place and become a factor in greater theatre enjoyment. He likewise soon becomes aware that the word *criticism* need not mean adverse, for the honest critic may also praise.

The cardinal rule for the beginner in dramatic criticism should be to have some good reason for whatever opinion he may express.

If he must present a written criticism, he should never tell the story. It is possible to tell the theme and maybe even what the play is about. At no time should any information be revealed that will mar the enjoyment for one who reads the criticism before seeing the event. This would mean, also, that the critic should take for granted that the reader has not seen the performance. It is always wise to avoid the use of technical or dramatic terms that are not generally known by the average reader.

A critic should always be as objective as possible in his reporting. Where emotion is involved, objectivity is very difficult, but the critic should at least report the reaction of the audience—especially if it has differed from his own. It is not his duty to say what should have been done, for he is not a creative artist. He is a reporter who also includes his own opinions on the artistic merits of the occasion. He need not mention everyone concerned, but should single out individual efforts that were outstanding in one way or another. Fundamentally, a critic is judging the play and the production on the basis of his own response or reactions to it. It is his duty to be didactic—to make up his mind—to speak his feelings, whatever they may be, honestly, forthrightly, sincerely. "The best dramatic criticism," Burns Mantle once said, "is like writing a letter home."

While a dramatic evaluation may carry more weight because it appears in the morning paper, and seem more authentic due to the prestige of the writer, it is not necessarily more honest or of greater value than that of the average theatregoer if that individual possesses some basic theatre knowledge and has conscientiously followed some honest set of principles on dramatic criticism.

VARIATIONS IN AUDIENCE AND CRITICAL ANALYSIS OF THE THREE MEDIUMS

The audience has already received considerable discussion in Chapter One. We would now further analyze this cosmopolitan and unpredictable element that so affects the total result of any given dramatic performance in the living theatre and, to a lesser degree, our reactions as a part of the audience at a motion picture or television program.

Psychologists have pointed out that audiences, in general, have certain qualities which make them different from individuals. This principle has been further treated by John Mason Brown[*] and also by Clayton Hamilton in his essay, "The Psychology of Audiences.[†] Each of these men has described the characteristics of an audience, and the following is a summation of the metamorphosis which takes place when the average man becomes part of an audience:

He loses his higher and more personal sensibilities of intellect or character;
. . . is less intellectual and more emotional;
. . . is less reasonable and judicious;
. . . descends several rungs in the ladder. He demands a struggle, is boyishly heroic, carelessly unthinking, easily credulous;
. . . wants to take sides, to hiss, or to applaud;
. . . finds that emotion is contagious, does what his neighbor does;
. . . is more sensuous, loves costumes, color, spectacle;

[*] John Mason Brown, *The Art of Playgoing* (New York: W. W. Norton, 1936).
[†] Clayton Hamilton, *Theory of the Theatre* (New York: Henry Holt & Co., 1939).

. . . is more commonplace; demands the love of woman, home, country, right;

. . . is more conservative;

. . . is a little hard of hearing;

. . . is unpredictable.

Any critical analysis of a dramatic production should take into account the audience present and its contributions to the total effect. This estimate should include our answers to the following questions: What sort of people in general make up the audience? What class do they represent chronologically, socially, and mentally? Have they come with the proper imaginary puissance or with the "show me" attitude? Have they displayed an interest and appreciation? Do they seem to understand the play and what the various artists are trying to do? Is this interest held throughout the performance? Is there a definite response of tears, laughter, applause, or silence? Are they emotionally moved, or bored? Do they cough, show restlessness, leave during the performance? Is the applause spontaneous, or politely perfunctory? To the people of what type, group, or age does the play make its greatest appeal? Would you advise your friends to see it and why?

So much for the audience itself and its difference from the individual in what it demands of a performance. Now for the effects of the audience in the preparation or the effect of an individual production. The immediacy of reaction and the awareness of that reaction on the part of the actors can have a great effect on any single stage dramatic event. Audience reactions are felt by the actors, and their performances—if ever so slightly—are altered in spite of their technical assurance. The temperature of the room, the weather, world conditions, headlines in the evening paper, the personnel of evening and matinee audiences, the night of the week, holiday crowds, and the varying personalities of the actors with their sensitivity to an audience reaction—all have an effect on any live stage performance. For this reason it is never quite fair to discuss the work of an actor unless those participating in that discussion have seen the same performance. This is even more unjust if it is the matter of a long run and it has been viewed early or late in that run. This, of course, is not true in a motion picture or television production.

Beyond the response of the audience and its effect on the actors, the stage and motion picture audience, in general, have more in common than does either with the television audience, but even they have their individual differences so far as the preparation of a production by playwright, actors, technicians and director are concerned.

Jean Cocteau has pointed out that the audience viewing a motion picture is seemingly enclosed with the actors in a room lacking a fourth wall. It has a feeling of equality with the actors that is lacking in the legitimate theatre when the players are observed as if through a keyhole. In the theatre there is a greater sense of detachment as the scene is outside the spectator. On the surface it would appear that this might make for greater empathy in the motion pictures. Undoubtedly this is partially true, since the films can show so much more detail and give at least the surface realism that may transport the audience physically as well as emotionally to the exact scene. It is unquestionably this ability which has greatly limited, if not eliminated, the use of imagination on the part of the audience in the motion picture theatre, whereas the imaginative element is one of the stage's greatest assets. While the cinema is far superior in its ability to picture realistic detail, it cannot compare with the stage in its illusion and imaginative qualities, or at least it has not done so.

The theatre audience is always conscious of flesh-and-blood actors, while in the motion picture, even in the peak of an emotion, there is always the consciousness of the inanimate. All of which means that in one the audience is primarily concerned with people and in the other primarily with pictures. Mr. Mamoulian has emphasized this point in his explanation of the great differences between stage and screen:

How often a shadow on the wall, a close-up of a door-knob, an ash tray or a crashed bottle can be as effective as the best acting. I have seen an Eleanora Duse or a Chaliapin, surrounded by pitiful mediocrities and shabby production, lift the evening in the theatre into the realm of exciting, unforgettable experiences through the sheer magic of their individual performances. But I have never seen a bad film saved by one performer. Indeed, the Stage is the kingdom of the actors, the Screen, the kingdom of the pictures.*

Few would debate the difference in mental age and attitude of the two theatres. A dearth of children attending one and the abundance of them in the other cannot but have its effect on both the artists who have prepared the play or picture and the audience reaction. This audience reaction is important in the individual critic's subconscious mind and does have its effect on his critical analysis. However, audience reaction in itself is not as important in the motion picture as in the theatre, for there, as has been pointed out, this reaction may affect the actors' performance and thus alter—if ever so slightly—the spirit or tone of the performance.

One needs only stand at a box office to see that hundreds of motion picture goers will purchase tickets and enter without even knowing what picture or actors they will see. This is a rare occasion in the legitimate theatre. In the first instance, they go to be going; in the second, they want to see that particular event. This fact alone has an inevitable influence on the audience. Furthermore, the avid followers of a given star are sometimes interested in his or her artistry, but more often are attracted by some physical appeal.

The motion picture, far more than the stage, is able to supply vicarious satisfaction to that "one-third of the nation who are ill-kept, ill-fed, and ill-housed." In the secluded darkness of the motion picture house these frustrated men and women, who have been denied the love, luxury, excitement, or emotional experiences their nature requires, may receive some measure of release and satisfaction. It is little wonder that the producers have tended to favor this huge audience, for the motion picture, as the professional stage or television, is also a business. It is likewise not surprising that their fundamental and principal appeal to the populace is based on

* Rouben Mamoulian, "Stage and Screen," *The Screen Writer,* March, 1947.

the element of sex, the most basic of human emotions. There are, of course, individuals of similar nature who seek their theatre in the legitimate houses, but the percentage is so much smaller that they do not receive the recognition given them by the motion picture producers.

An additional item of difference is the matter of censorship. The motion pictures must unfortunately abide by the moral code of some omnipotent group whose approach to the diety has, by the grace of a political appointment, given them the power to decide what is good and what is bad in the world. They sit in judgment and decide what is moral enough for their fellow men to see, and what they delete often makes one wonder by what quirk of the mind they could have found evil where few others can see it. Save in an occasional instance, the stage has not suffered such humiliation.

The very important matter of coordinating the audience reaction with that of the production and thus establishing the correct rhythm is almost impossible in the motion picture due to the wide range of audiences, both in size and response. We sense it when, with a full house at a comedy or farce, we miss many lines due to the laughter, or in a partially empty house, the lack of an expected response again destroys the basic rhythm.

One of the major contrasts is the difference of appeal—that of the motion picture is principally to sight and that of the stage more to hearing, although as has been pointed out, the latter throws more emphasis on sight than ever before. Mr. Mamoulian has said:

The essence of a picture is and always will be the visual. A motion picture does not exist for a blind man, no matter how well he can hear the words . . . We are using too much dialogue on the screen. The formula should be: express everything in the visual image and movement, and only when these are inadequate, use spoken words.*

Professor Allardyce Nicoll has emphasized the same note by saying:

* Rouben Mamoulian, "Stage and Screen," *The Screen Writer,* March, 1947

Whereas in general a stage play demands constant talk, a film requires an absolute minimum of words. The essential basis of the cinema lies primarily in the realm of the visual images.

This comes home more vividly when we recall how easy it is to follow a foreign film even when we do not know the language.

Perhaps the greatest single difference between television and the two other mediums is in its audience. We are not now concerned with those in the broadcasting studio, but rather the individuals viewing the performance before millions of receiving sets. There may be one, two, three or any number located in homes, bars, restaurants, service clubs, hotel lobbies, or wherever people may be gathered before a television set. Their ages, background, state of health, experience, and demands run the gamut, more varied than for either the stage or cinema. Even the time of day is not constant. A program wholly satisfactory for adults at ten o'clock in New York could be displeasing to the seven o'clock children's audience in California. Each television artist must think of himself as an additional guest in each of these groups, but the generosity usually afforded a guest cannot be depended upon, for the program can be abruptly ended at any moment.

In spite of this wide variety of viewers, the producers are well aware that the vast majority of their audience is at home. They also know that there is no more personal or intimate relationship possible. Each member of such an audience is completely free from the sophistications or pretenses he may don when in contact with the outside world or when part of a crowd. A man alone is sincere, and he demands the same sincerity and truthfulness from every aspect of the television production. He may wish the drama or comedy to be amusing, shocking, frightening, mysterious, or exciting, but it must present unmistakable truth, whether in the imagination of fantasy or in the characterizations of realistic theatre.

It is far easier to detect falseness and cheapness under these intimate circumstances, for the characteristics of an audience which differentiate it from the individual are no longer present. The viewer is not swayed by his neighbor nor by a feeling that he must like what he should like. As a further disadvantage his interests are divided. There are the distractions of the home which are never present in the theatre—the telephone, visitors, letting out the dog, watching the baby, attending the furnace. These interruptions all play a part in his over-all evaluation of the program.

To criticize justly we must always ask if this is a live or a taped (or filmed) program. The live show is more limited in its dramatic time (that period covered by the story's action) as well as in costume or set changes. It has the possibility of human error, but it also holds the excitement of the "future becoming the past" before our eyes. The film with its greater variety and fluidity has eliminated all possibilities of error, and as in the cinema, we merely watch the "past become the present." Frequently there are parts of each which complicate judgment somewhat.

There is an additional advantage and responsibility that is peculiarly ours as members of a television audience. This is the immediacy and the tremendous effect that our reactions can have on the sponsors and on the broadcaster. The air which carries any program into our homes belongs not to the station nor to the producer, but to *us*. We need only voice our complaint or our praise. Vast millions see a program on a single evening. It would take months or years for the same number to see any given cinema or stage production. What was said earlier about the power of the audience is more poignant in television than in any other medium. Truly the calibre of television entertainment lies largely in our hands, for the program that emanates from any studio can be of our choosing. It behooves us all to choose wisely and with discrimination and above all to make our desires known.

Any honest evaluation of television will find the vast majority of programs must be approached on the third level of dramatic criticism—which we have defined as "show business." We may rationalize or wish for more, but by its very nature it must appeal to the mass audience. Bound by all its purely commercial restrictions, the necessity of appealing to many, time limitations, available material, expense of production, necessity for financial return on investment, we must accept the fact that television *is* show business. This does not mean that it should not strive to be the very best of its kind, and it is the duty of an intelligent audience to demand just that! Frequently a program does rise to the second level of criticism by creating the theatre magic or aesthetic enjoyment that that level implies. Our overt praise of such an effort can bring more of the same. Occasionally, the medium has really distinguished itself and by so doing demanded that it be considered on the highest level of dramatic criticism. It is on these all too rare occasions that our joy and enthusiasm is dampened only by the extremely low audience response as reflected by the professional ratings.

Due to these differences in both the audience and the techniques of the motion picture and television, there are a few specific items that should be given special attention in their dramatic criticism. We would specifically cite the use of the close-up, medium or long shot, unusual camera angles, cinematic effects, music or sound used to establish or maintain a mood, introduce a situation, establish locale, identify character or background. We should recognize the use of photography and background rather than dialogue to project story, ideas, situations, or characterization, and finally, we should note whatever difference there may be in the over-all interpretation of life being projected which is peculiar to the specific medium being used.

In conclusion we would present ten items we believe should be incorporated in any honest dramatic criticism. The first five are concerned with the critic himself and have incorporated both the obligations of an audience and the requisites of a dramatic critic as they have been previously discussed. The second five are concerned with the work of the various artists involved in the production. All ten draw upon the facts, principles and opinions that have been expressed on the preceding pages in an effort to explain the substance, form and technique of those who make up the theatre—playwright, actors, technicians, director, and audience. The application of these ten statements should bring forth an intelligent and honest evaluation of a dramatic production in any of the three dramatic mediums.

TEN COMMANDMENTS OF DRAMATIC CRITICISM

1. *I must* constantly—in all my theatre experience—use imaginary puissance.

2. *I must* know, understand, evaluate and discount my own prejudices.

3. *I must* evaluate each of the five areas and the work of all artists involved in the production.

4. *I must* measure the entire production in terms of life and understand what each artist has personally contributed through and of himself to make or mar the production.

5. *I must* arrive at every decision only after using Goethe's three principles of artistic criticism.

6. *Each and every artist* must make crystal clear what he is trying to say through proper emphasis, sincerity and technique.

7. *Each and every artist* must work within the medium at hand or successfully adapt any elements borrowed from another medium.

8. *Each and every artist* must cooperate and coordinate his work toward a single goal which is, in turn, the theme or the purpose of the production.

9. *Each and every artist* must seem real and be wholly believable in his contribution to this production that is a work of art; in short, each must give me a picture of life interpreted through his personality.

10. *In the final analysis* the production may move me, stir me, excite me, amuse me, teach me, or transform me, but the one thing it *dare not do* is to bore me. The one thing it *must do* is send me on my way somehow better equipped to face Life.

All the verbs used in commandment number ten have been carefully chosen, for it is a basic tenet of our particular theory of dramatic criticism that the theatre exists on several planes and can be many things to many people. There is ample room in our world of theatre for both *Ten Little Indians* and *Waiting for Godot,* for *Auntie Mame* and *Long Day's Journey Into Night,* for *Charley's Aunt* and *Mother Courage,* for *Three Men on a Horse* and *Hamlet,* for *Blithe Spirit* and *Oedipus Rex,* and for all the levels that lie in between.

As individuals we might prefer the theatre that gives us more than mere escape, but at times we might also profit from some purely escapist dramatic fare. We might favor the theatre that is a teacher and an art, but we would not dismiss that which only attempts to amuse or to excite. The release of these emotions can also send us on our way better equipped to face life.

Glossary of theatre terms

Most of the following terms are frequently used in discussions involving the stage, motion picture, or television. A knowledge of their meaning is essential. Generally, those which were defined or discussed in the text have not been included here.

ABSTRACT SET. Drapes, single units of doors or windows arranged for music or ballet numbers. No effort at realism or locale. Common in television.

ACTORS' EQUITY ASSOCIATION. Union of professional legitimate theatre actors with headquarters in New York City.

A.F.T.R.A. American Federation of Television and Radio Artists. Union for television and radio actors with offices in New York City and Los Angeles.

ANGEL. Individual who furnishes financial backing for a production, whose name rarely appears in connection with it.

A.N.T.A. American National Theatre and Academy. Congressionally chartered organization for serving the theatre in all its branches. Supplies advice and various services. Offices in New York City.

ANNIE OAKLEY. A pass or complimentary ticket to the theatre, so called because of the habit of punching holes in such a ticket in the pre-rubber stamp days.

ANTAGONIST. The character most in opposition to main character (protagonist) of the play.

ANTOINETTE PERRY AWARDS. "Tonies," awarded each season for outstanding work in writing, acting, and design in the New York theatre. An award in honor of the late Antoinette Perry, actress and director.

APRON. Space on stage in front of main curtain; very wide in Restoration and eighteenth century. Much of the play took place here.

ARENA STAGE. A form of center staging with audience on three or four sides. (See "Theatre-in-the-round" and "Penthouse theatre.")

ARRAS SETTING. Half circle of neutral draperies which serve as formal background for the stage. (See "Cyclorama.")

ARTISTIC FAILURE. Play that may have artistic qualities but has received poor notices and is a failure at the box office.

ASIDE. Words spoken by the actor in a lower tone. The audience, but not the other characters of the play, is supposed to hear them.

AUDIO. Sound portion of a television show.

GLOSSARY OF THEATRE TERMS

BACKDROP. Large flat surface at rear of stage, painted to suggest locale and used with wings in seventeenth, eighteenth, and nineteenth centuries. In present-day theatre usually represents sky. (See "Skydrop.")

BACKING. A series of flats or drops placed behind doors and windows to mask backstage area.

BACKSTAGE. The entire area behind the proscenium arch, but normally during the action of the play that area which is not seen by the audience.

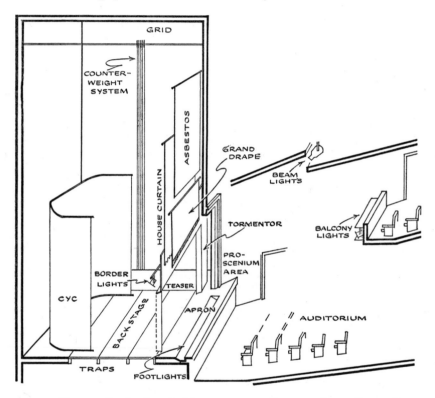

BIT PART. Very small role, described by one actor as "two speeches and a spit," such as "The carriage awaits, milady."

BLOOPER. Error by some member of cast or crew. Sometimes called "goof" or "boo-boo."

BORDER. A short curtain hung above the stage to mask the flies when a ceiling piece is not being used.

BORDERLIGHTS. A series of lights above and at front of stage to light the acting area with general illumination.

BOX SET. Standard setting of today with back wall, two side walls, and usually a ceiling to represent the interior of a room.

BROAD COMEDY. Slapstick bordering on farce or burlesque. Overdone for sake of "groundlings," and lacking subtlety.

BRIDGE. A transition from one scene to another. In radio it is usually music; on television the use of a small object such as a letter, picture, or fan to allow change from one set to the other by an actor.

BURLESQUE. An exaggeration in character traits, stage business, or movement, so overdone that the sense of reality or its illusion are destroyed. Emphasizes humor.

CHEAT. To turn body or play toward audience while appearing to be in conversation with other players on the stage.

CLAMBAKE. A poorly constructed or rehearsed program that is much below standard.

CLAQUE. A group in the audience (friends or especially hired) who applaud or react vocally to give the impression of great enthusiasm for the performance.

COMMEDIA DELL' ARTE. A pantomime or drama without any set literary form. The theatre of common people in Europe beginning with the fifteenth century. It gave us such characters as Harlequin, Pierrot, Columbine, etc.

CONVENTIONAL THEATRE. Indicates accepted theatre building with raised stage, scenery, lights, and proscenium, with auditorium and audience out front as we know it.

CRITIC'S CIRCLE. A group composed of all first-line New York critics for newspapers and magazines (about twenty-eight) who by secret ballot award prizes to best American and foreign play and musical each spring.

CROSS-FADE. **Audio**—to fade out one sound and fade another in. **Video**—to fade out one picture and face another in.

CUE. The final words, business, or movement of one character before another begins his own.

CUT. **Stage**—to delete a line or omit certain business. **Screen**—transference from one picture to another.

CYCLORAMA OR "CYC." Curtain or canvas usually hung in half-circle to cover back and sides of stage. May represent blue of sky or be plain drape setting. (**See** "Arras setting.")

DÉCOR. Furnishings, properties, draperies, and decorations of setting. (**See** "Inscenierung.")

DÉNOUEMENT. The moment when the last suspense is eliminated. From the French—literal translations is "untying of the last knot." Usually comes with or after climax and before conclusion.

"DEUS EX MACHINA." **See** "God from the machine."

DISSOLVE. The second shot appears on the screen under the first and becomes in-increasingly distinct as the first disappears. Serves to connect scenes on the screen.

DOWNSTAGE. The part of the stage nearest the audience.

DRAMATIC TIME. The period that elapses in the action of a script. (**See** "Physical time.")

DRESSING THE HOUSE. Scattering the audience by leaving pairs or more of seats empty to give impression of a larger attendance.

DROP. The name given the curtains that are hung from the flies.

DRY-RUN. Full rehearsal without the use of cameras.

EMMY. Television award given annually. (See "Oscar.")

FADE-IN AND FADE-OUT. Light intensity of first camera shot falls to zero and second rises to normal value. Serves to disconnect scenes.

FILM CLIP. Film inserted into a live telecast.

FILTER. Audio effect used to give a metallic quality to the voice, such as talking over telephone.

FLAT. A piece of scenery composed of muslin, canvas, or linen stretched over a wooden frame. Used for walls or backing of a set.

FLIES. The whole area above stage back of the proscenium where borders, drops, and small pieces of scenery are hung.

FLUFFED LINE. A stammer, stutter, twisting of words, or other faulty delivery by the actor.

FLY. To raise scenery above the floor of the stage by use of ropes, battens, etc.

FLY CATCHING. Movement, business, or sound made by an actor to attract attention to himself when emphasis should be elsewhere.

FORESTAGE. Part of stage nearest audience when an inner proscenium is used. Sometimes used interchangeably with "apron."

FORMAT. Style or make-up of a television script. Also used to describe the method or pattern of opening and closing the program. Usually followed from week to week.

47 WORKSHOP. Playwriting course originally at Harvard and later at Yale under George Pierce Baker. Gave us many leading playwrights of the twentieth century.

FREEZE. To stand completely still as if for a picture.

GEORGE SPELVIN. Name often used by an actor for the second or lesser role he is playing. Sometimes credited to William Gillette, William Collier, Sr., and William Seymour, but generally accepted to have been used for the first time in 1907 in Winchell Smith's and Frederic Thompson's play, **Brewster's Millions**. An actor chose the name for a second role. The critics praised "George Spelvin" for his work and the play was a hit. Smith always insisted on listing the same name on future programs, for luck.

GHOST WALKS. Used by actors to denote payday.

GIMMICK. A device or trick used for a special effect, usually in an effort to get a laugh, although it may seek any emotion.

GOD FROM THE MACHINE. From the Latin, "deus ex machina," when Fate (or the author) intercedes to save the action from the logical conclusion.

GOOD THEATRE. A quality that makes a play especially effective when presented before an audience.

GRAND DRAPE. A curtain above the stage and at the top of the proscenium arch; it hangs in front of the main curtain and decorates the top of the stage and reduces the height of the opening.

GRIDIRON OR GRID. Framework of wood or steel above the stage. Used to support and fly scenery.

GROUND CLOTH. Waterproof canvas covering usually used to cover the entire stage floor.

GROUNDLINGS. Term used by Shakespeare to indicate the uneducated and untrained theatregoers who sat in the pit, and were highly entertained by broad comedy.

GROUND ROW. Profile at the back of stage representing trees, shrubbery, hills, etc. Masks the meeting of stage floor and cyclorama.

HAM ACTING. An exaggerated and insincere performance, notable for noise rather than honest feeling or sincerity. Extravagant gestures, choking sounds, and trickery are used for their effect alone. Should not be confused with broad acting or projection.

HOKUM. Deliberate simulation of emotion by artificial means, and also the means used. Sure-fire but time-worn theatrical tricks.

HOUSE SEATS. Seats retained by the management to cover errors or to be given to distinguished guests. Released just before curtain time.

IDIOT-SHEET. Copy, cue lines, or other material written in large letters for television actors, announcers, or others.

IMAGE. Picture appearing on the television screen.

INNER STAGE. In Elizabethan theatre the small area upstage and enclosed by curtains. It localized action which moved forward to outer stage after the scene was underway.

INSCENIERUNG. German term to indicate the whole visual stage picture, including lighting. (See "Décor.")

LIGHT LEAK. Light that can be seen through a crack or opening in the set.

LIGHT SPILL. Light that strikes the proscenium or set and thus "spills over" in a distracting manner, rather than striking just the area it is supposed to cover.

LIVE. Actually present in studio, as opposed to filmed or recorded.

LOCK. Term indicating those elements which prevent a character from escaping the results of the conflict.

MASK. To cover from view of the audience with some type of scenery.

MONTAGE. A rapid series of different pictures that build to a climax and in doing so give a single impression.

MOSCOW ART THEATRE. Established by Constantin Stanislavsky in the last decade of the nineteenth century, and until the Stalin regime considered one of the finest theatres in the world.

MUFF. To mispronounce or transpose words or syllables.

MUSICAL COMEDY. A light story with spoken dialogue interspersed with music and dances.

OBLIGATORY SCENE. The scene of the play which the playwright has led us to expect and without which the audience would be disappointed. Sometimes referred to as "scène-à-faire."

OSCAR. Motion Picture Academy Award, given each year for the outstanding achievement in all phases of the cinema.

OUTER STAGE. Forestage of Elizabethan theatre and used especially for soliloquies and most dramatic scenes. Historically preceded the apron. (See "Apron.")

PAN. To criticize adversely. Screen—Relates to camera angle as it moves from one position to another without a break.

PAPER. Complimentary tickets given out free or at reduced rates to bring in a larger audience. Sometimes called "papering the house."

PENTHOUSE THEATRE. Name given to the first arena theatre of this century when it opened at the University of Washington.

PERIPETEIA OR PERIPETY. A reversal of circumstances which leads to a result contrary to our expectation.

PHYSICAL TIME. The actual minute length of the production, as opposed to the dramatic time.

PLANT. Apparently casual insertion of an idea, character, or property to be used more significantly later in the play.

PLASTIC SCENERY. Built in three dimensions rather than being painted on a flat surface.

PLAYWRIGHTS COMPANY. A producing organization in New York controlled principally by playwrights themselves. The founding members (1938) were S. N. Behrman, Maxwell Anderson, Robert Sherwood, Sidney Howard, and Elmer Rice.

"THE POETICS." Written by Aristotle (360-322 B.C.). The earliest critical treatise extant dealing with dramatic practice and theory.

POINT OF ATTACK. That arbitrary point where the writer has chosen to begin his script.

PRACTICAL. Scenery that is usable; a door or window that will open, etc.

PRODUCER. In America the individual or group who raises the money or underwrites the production financially. In England usually considered to be the director as well.

PROJECT OR PROJECTION. Stage—To increase size of voice, movement, and gesture so it can be seen and heard in the rear of the auditorium. It "theatricalizes nature," so to speak, by increasing the feeling, but all is done with sincerity. Sometimes called "playing broadly," but not to be confused with "ham acting." Screen— Throwing the picture on the screen.

PROPERTIES OR PROPS. Any article or piece of furniture used by the actor.

PROSCENIUM. The wall that separates the audience from the backstage.

PROSCENIUM ARCH. The opening in the proscenium through which the audience sees the stage; the picture frame.

PROTAGONIST. The leading character in the play—the one in whom the audience is most interested.

PULITZER PRIZE. Award given each year to the best play on an American theme.

RAKE. To place the set on a slant. Usually applied to side walls.

REPERTOIRE, OR REPERTORY. A list of dramas, operas, parts, etc., which a company or person has rehearsed and is prepared to perform. They are alternated in performance.

REPERTORY COMPANY. Theatrical group that has and performs a repertoire.

RESOLUTION. Method of solving all conflicts presented in the play.

RETURN. A flat used at extreme right and left of stage and running off stage behind the tormentor. Sometimes it serves as the tormentor.

REVUE. A series of unrelated songs, skits, dances, very loosely tied together by the title—usually some topical subject. All pretense of plot is abandoned.

SCENARIO. General description of action for a proposed motion picture.

SCÈNE-À-FAIRE. (See "Obligatory scene.")

SCHMALTZ. Overly sentimental material, usually with the use of music in the background. Sometimes applied to overacting or production.

SCREEN ACTORS GUILD. Union of motion picture actors.

SCRIPT. The written drama from which the play is built.

SET PIECES. Scenery that will stand without support. Used especially in nonrealistic productions.

SHOW BUSINESS. Name applied to theatre productions pandering to a nondiscerning audience and emphasizing escape or box-office appeal rather than literary or theatrical merit.

SKELETON SETTING. Rudiments of a setting, appealing largely to the imagination of the audience.

SKENE. A small hut in the Greek theatre, used for concealment during a change of costume. It has given us the English word "scene."

SKIT. A short scene of dialogue or pantomime, usually in a satirical or humorous vein.

SKY-DROP. A drop painted blue to represent sky and to mask rear of stage; hangs from the flies. (See "Cyclorama.")

SNEAK. To bring in music, sound, or voices at an extremely low level of volume.

SNOW. White spots or interference in television picture. Due to low level of the station broadcasting.

SOLILOQUY. A speech delivered by the actor when alone on the stage. There are two types:

Constructive—to explain the plot to the audience, as in many of Shakespeare's prologues.

Reflective—to show personal thought or emotion, as in **Hamlet.**

STAGE RIGHT AND LEFT. Right or left side of the stage from the actor's point of view.

STATIC PLAY. One in which very little happens and the characters and situations are essentially the same at the end as in the beginning.

STEAL. Getting from one part of the stage to another without its being noticed. Also applied to taking a scene that really belongs to another.

STING. To punctuate with a sudden musical phrase, shout, or some other emphatic sound.

STOCK, STOCK COMPANY. A resident company presenting a series of plays, each for a limited run, but not repeated after that engagement.

SUPERIMPOSE. Overlapping of two picture frames. The images of two cameras seen together, one on top of the other.

TAG. Final line of the play.

TEASER. Border just upstage and back of the front curtain. Masks the flies and determines the height of the proscenium opening during the performance.

THEATRE GUILD. Producing organization in New York. It works on a subscription series there and in many other large cities.

THEATRE-IN-THE-ROUND. (See "Arena stage.")

THE THÉÂTRE LIBRE (Paris). Free theatre in France in 1887. Headed by André Antoine, it introduced Naturalism and freedom from the artificiality of the nineteenth century.

"THE METHOD." Name applied to the Russian or Stanislavsky approach to acting; very subjective, introspective, and individualistic.

TORMENTORS. Flats at extreme down right and left of stage near proscenium and masking backstage area. (See "Return.")

TRAP. Opening in stage floor, permitting entrances or exits from under the floor.

TURKEY. Name indicating the dramatic production that has utterly failed.

UNIT SETTING. Pieces of scenery—flats, pillars, doors, pylons, arches, etc.—that can be put together in various combinations to furnish different settings.

UPSTAGE. Toward back of stage. For many years the stage was higher in the back and slanted down toward the footlights and audience. This is still true in some European theatres.

VICTORIAN. Applied to the era of Queen Victoria or the second half of the nineteenth century in England. Noted for prudery and ostentation in art.

VIDEO. The sight portion of a television program.

WASHINGTON SQUARE PLAYERS. Amateur group, which grew into the present successful Theatre Guild.

WELL-MADE PLAY. A name given those plays written in mid-nineteenth century which followed a set pattern or formula in their construction. Now has a derogatory meaning.

WINGS. Off-stage space to left and right. Sometimes refers to wing pieces used in series of two or three on either side of stage as part of wing and backdrop set.

WIPE. First camera shot is peeled off, revealing the second as if it had previously been there.

ZOOM. A camera movement toward or away from the object—very fast and smooth.